Beyond Basic
FLY TYING

Beyond Basic
FLY TYING

Techniques and Patterns to Expand Your Skills

Jon Rounds, *editor*

Marvin Nolte,
fly tier and consultant

Photographs by
Michael Radencich

STACKPOLE
BOOKS

Copyright © 2008 by Stackpole Books

Published by
STACKPOLE BOOKS
5067 Ritter Road
Mechanicsburg, PA 17055
www.stackpolebooks.com

Printed in China

10 9 8 7 6 5 4 3 2 1

First edition

Illustrations by John McKim

Library of Congress Cataloging-in-Publication Data

Beyond basic fly tying : techniques and patterns to expand your skills / Jon Rounds, editor ; Marvin Nolte, fly tier and consultant ; photographs by Michael Radencich. — 1st ed.
    p. cm.
ISBN-13: 978-0-8117-3450-9
ISBN-10: 0-8117-3450-1
1. Fly tying. I. Rounds, Jon.

SH451.B47 2008
688.7'9124—dc22

2007040346

Contents

Introduction

This book is for tiers who know the basics and are ready to move on to patterns that demand more skill. We assume you know how to start thread on a hook, apply dubbing, stack hair, and wind hackle. We further assume that you want to tie flies to catch fish rather than to occupy your time with craft projects, and these premises guide both the content of the book and the method of instruction.

As to the content, we chose patterns that have been proven producers and that experienced fly fishers carry. We avoided patterns with narrow or local applications, or those that merely look pretty or include a neat little tying trick. We also wanted patterns that as a group would fill a trout fisherman's needs in every situation. Thus, the book includes flies from each category— nymphs, wet flies/emergers, dry flies, terrestrials, and streamers. The first three categories are presented in an order that reflects the life cycle of aquatic insects in their journey from stream bottom to top. Finally, each group represents the array of tying skills most essential to its category. For example, the patterns in our dry fly section will teach you how to make the upright wings of a Catskill dry, how to wind parachute hackle around a wingpost, how to make the wings of a caddis pattern, and so on, so that when you finish the patterns in this section, you'll be well equipped to tie just about any dry fly.

As to the method of instruction, we've observed that most tiers learn technique most efficiently in context, that is, by tying flies. Rather than sitting down and practicing isolated skills, such as making upright dry fly wings or spinning deer hair, most of us prefer to learn such moves by tying Light Cahills and Muddler Minnows. Therefore, after an introductory chapter on tools and materials, this book gets quickly to the business at hand: tying flies.

1

Tools and Materials

TOOLS

Progressing from basic fly tying to more advanced patterns and techniques does not necessarily mean acquiring more tools. Many experts actually *reduce* the number of gadgets in their kit as they develop their skills, focusing instead on higher-quality models of essential tools or ones that fit them comfortably. This principle is particularly true of the two most essential tools: the vise and scissors.

VISE

Most expert tiers use rotary vises. If you began tying with an inexpensive stationary vise and now tie regu-

larly, the next logical step is a high-quality rotary. The rotary feature gives you quick and easy access to the underside of the fly for steps such as trimming dubbing and applying cement, and it also allows you to view an entire fly from every angle without removing it from the vise. In addition, if you plan to tie patterns with epoxy bodies, as many saltwater flies do, a rotary vise lets you rotate the fly while the epoxy is drying to create a smoothly shaped body.

But beware—inexpensive rotary vises with many features may lack the quality materials and precise machining necessary for a vise's most essential function:

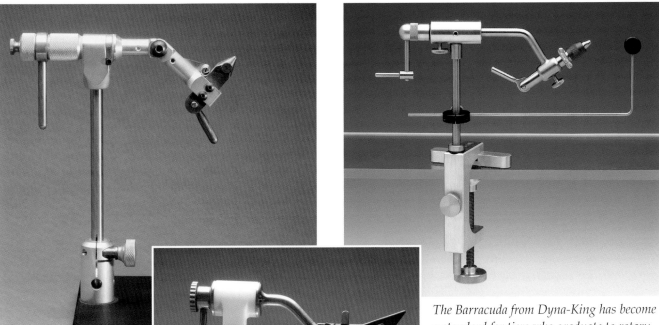

The Renzetti Master is a high-end rotary vise, about $630, used by many experts and professionals.

The Barracuda from Dyna-King has become a standard for tiers who graduate to rotary vises. This is the Deluxe model, with brass knobs and appointments.

Marvin Nolte uses a LAW Bench Vise, handmade by Lawrence A. Waldron of Seisdon, England.

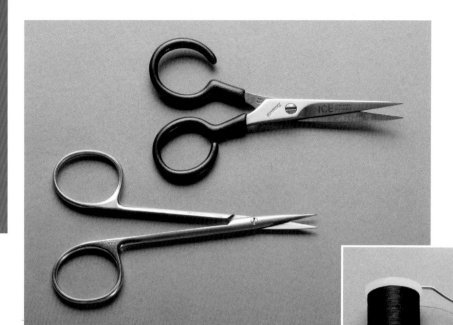

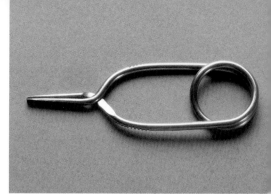

English-style hackle pliers are a simple and practical design. Avoid miniature models.

Keep two pairs of scissors at hand, one for tying (bottom) and one with heavier, serrated blades for cutting coarse material and wire.

Bobbins are available with ceramic tubes (top) or steel tubes. The ceramic models resist scoring by thread and thus last longer.

holding a hook securely. High-quality vises begin with precision-machined steel jaws that can hold very small (20 and down) to very large (1/0 and up) hooks securely and without damage. This function, in turn, demands precise mating of jaws and a finely adjustable tightening system. Different designers achieve these goals in different ways, but all top-quality vises perform the basics flawlessly.

The choice of vise, as with any fine tool, involves some subjectivity. A design that one tier finds comfortable, another tier finds clumsy. An accessory that gets in the way of one tier, another can't live without. The best approach is to try out a vise at a fly shop or at a friend's house. See what feels right.

Then again, if you're happy with your stationary vise, there's no need to buy a new one. No pattern in this book requires a rotary vise, and keep in mind that many expert tiers still use the stationary vise.

SCISSORS

Buy the best scissors you can afford. No tool is used more, and none will have more effect on the ease of your tying and the quality of your product. Most expert tiers wear their scissors as they tie, rather than putting them on and taking them off. Thus, the scissors must be

comfortable, and since different models and brands have different size finger loops, it makes sense to try on a pair before you buy.

The blades of tying scissors must of course be sharp and hold an edge, but their tips should also mate perfectly so you can cut material precisely using the very end of the scissors.

Light-gauge weighting wire is soft enough to cut with tying scissors without damaging them, but whenever you use these scissors for coarser material, use the base of the blades rather than the tips. Save the tips for the finest work.

You'll want a second, heavier pair of scissors, preferably with serrated blades, for cutting coarse and tough material, such as wire, coarse animal hair, and some synthetics, which can dull fine tying scissors. This second pair of scissors need not be costly.

BOBBINS

Bobbins don't require much thought. Models from any established maker will do. You will have to choose between steel or ceramic tubes. Ceramic tubes are more durable: they don't become grooved over time, as steel tubes can, but they are also more expensive.

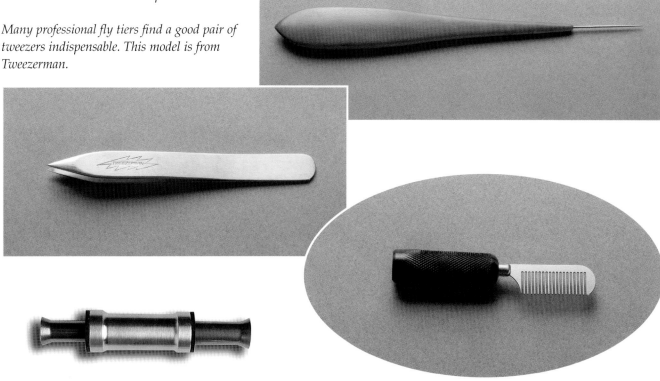

The many uses for a bodkin include manipulating fine material and dabbing on head cement. It need not be expensive.

Many professional fly tiers find a good pair of tweezers indispensable. This model is from Tweezerman.

If you buy just one hair stacker, get a combination model that takes longer hair in one end and shorter hair in the other.

A small, fine-toothed comb is useful for combing the underfur from clumps of deer and other animal hair before stacking.

Whatever model you choose, buy several. Experts and professionals keep a drawer full of bobbins loaded with the sizes and colors of thread they use most, so when they move from one pattern to the next, they don't have to rethread a bobbin each time.

HACKLE PLIERS
Hackle pliers need not be expensive, but they should have jaws that mate precisely and with enough tension to hold hackle firmly without damaging it.

Avoid the plastic-handled electrical-lead clips, sometimes included in beginner's kits as hackle pliers; they're almost useless for gripping hackle, though they come in handy for holding material out of the way when you're working on other parts of a pattern. Like-wise, avoid cheap pliers with jagged jaws that can damage hackle tips. You should also avoid miniature hackle pliers; they're not as easy to handle as normal-size models and don't have enough weight to dangle and hold wrapped hackle or other material in place.

TWEEZERS
Tweezers are not included in many kits, but many professionals would never be without a pair. You can use

them to manage stray wisps of material on an almost-finished fly, especially very small patterns with material too fine to manipulate with fingers. They're also handy for picking up and positioning small items, such as beads and tiny hooks. Many pros use the Tweezerman brand, which can be found in the cosmetic department of pharmacies and department stores, or online.

BODKIN
Any design will do, but a bodkin is handy for teasing out wisps of dubbing, applying flexible cement, and dozens of other incidental tasks.

HAIR STACKER
It's useful to have hair stackers in a few different sizes. If you buy only one, make it a combination model that takes longer hair in one end and shorter hair in the other.

One technique tip for stacking hair: to make the tips align quickly, rap the stacker sharply—not gently—a few times on your bench. Also, remember that hair with the underfur removed is much easier to stack. A small, fine-toothed comb is helpful for cleaning the underfur from a patch of hair.

DUBBING BLENDERS

A wide array of blended dubbing is available from fly-tying retailers. Randall Kaufmann and Dave Whitlock are two of the more well-known tiers who have developed dubbing blends for their patterns. Using commercial blends will save you time if you prefer, although one step in becoming an advanced tier is mixing your own blends. You can experiment with natural and synthetic materials to match the bodies of insects on your home water or to duplicate someone else's patterns.

Small amounts of dubbing can be blended by hand by cutting lengths of hair from a hide or lengths of synthetic fibers from a bundle, pulling the individual strands apart, and then mixing them up with your fingers. Many effective blends are mixes of flashy synthetic fibers, like Antron, and natural hair.

You can use a coffee grinder to mix larger amounts of dubbing—enough for a few flies, say. Place the clumps of hair or synthetics in the grinder and tap the switch five or six times, leaving it on for just a second each time.

For mixing large amounts of dubbing—for tying a single pattern by the dozen, for example—you can use a blender instead of a coffee grinder. Note, though, that you will need a substantial amount of material to blend the material effectively. Too little material won't mix—it will just get blown around.

MATERIALS

Entire books have been written on fly-tying materials, and this introductory section is not intended to be comprehensive; it will instead draw attention to key features in the most important materials. It will also serve as a guide to buying the materials used in the patterns in this book, as well as a reference if you have questions about materials described in tying instructions. We begin with a review of the two most basic materials: hooks and thread.

HOOKS

Never buy cheap hooks. They may be made from inferior steel and machined less precisely than quality hooks. They may break in the vise or on the water, they may rust when stored in the box, and their points may not be as sharp as those on good hooks or may become dull more quickly.

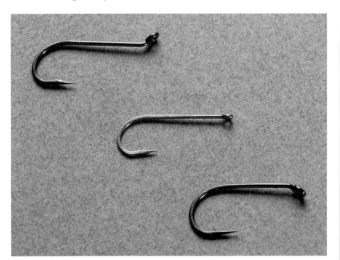

Hook-eye types, from top: up-eye, straight, and down-eye. The down-eye is by far the most widely used style for flies, but for reasons that pertain more to fishing than to tying: This type is handiest for threading a tippet through and for tying knots to.

Mustad and Tiemco are just two manufacturers of high-quality fly-tying hooks. The flies in this book and accompanying DVD, except as noted, were tied on Mustad Signature hooks, an excellent hook at a reasonable price. Expert tiers have personal preferences, and some like models by different manufacturers for different patterns. But all experienced tiers use established brands.

Handling and storage tip: Don't put a damp fly back in the box. Moisture promotes rust on the hook and also shortens the life of fly materials. When you change patterns on the stream, stick the fly you've just removed on a vest patch until it dries. If the whole box gets dunked and it's not watertight, let it sit on the car seat with the lid open on the drive home, and then, if the flies still aren't dry, spread them out on a paper towel until they are.

Hook Nomenclature

The following terms are basic, but so essential to following tying directions and making well-proportioned flies that we include them here. Internalizing the relationships between hook parts and fly parts is one of the skills of an advanced tier.

"Shank" is not only a general term for the main shaft of the hook; it is also a specific dimension significant in tying directions—the length of the shaft from the rear of the eye to a point directly above the point of the barb. The lengths of certain fly parts, such as wings and tails, are expressed in terms of shank length. For example, a tail might need to be 1 shank or ½ shank long. Likewise, directions on where to stop or start winding thread or material are often given in terms of shank-length: "advance the thread to the one-third point," for example, means to advance the thread to a point ⅓ shank-length from the eye.

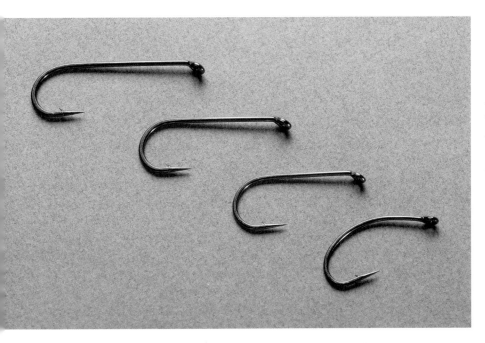

*Hook types, from top:
4X long streamer,
2X stout (standard wet or nymph),
1X fine (standard dry fly),
curved scud.*

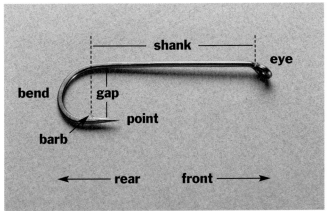

The hook's shank-length and gap are used repeatedly as references in tying directions to specify the size of fly parts, and a well-proportioned fly shows attention to this relationship. Note the significant difference between the hook's overall length and its shank-length. Also remember that in tying directions, "forward" means toward the eye and "rearward" toward the bend.

The "gap" is another hook part used as a reference for fly dimensions; you may be told to select hackle with barbs 1½ times as long as the gap, or to make a wing case 1 gap wide.

A well-made fly shows close attention to the proportions dictated by the hook. In other words, a skilled tier adjusts the length and diameter of materials using the hook's shank-length and gap for reference to create realistic and well-proportioned patterns.

Hook Length and Weight

For each hook size, there is a "standard" length as well as longer and shorter versions. Variations in length are expressed by a number and an "X" that signifies how much longer the hook is than standard. For example, a

size 14 "1X long" dry fly hook is a bit longer than a size 14 standard dry fly hook, a "2X long," longer still. Streamer hooks are typically "3X" or "4X long," because streamers imitate baitfish, whose bodies are longer than most insects'. Conversely, a "1X short" hook is a bit shorter than standard and is used for tying stubby nymphs and the like.

The same system applies to the thickness of the hook wire. A "1X fine" hook is a little lighter gauge wire than standard, and a "1X heavy" ("strong" or "stout") a bit heavier. A standard dry fly hook is "1X fine," because dry flies must be buoyant. Wet fly or nymph hooks are typically "1X" or "2X heavy," because these flies must sink. You should expect slight variations in size between models from different makers, however, as there is no universal set of standards used by all hook manufacturers.

THREAD

Because thread is handled constantly, is under tension throughout the tying process, and is the principal material holding the fly together in the water, it makes no sense to use anything but a high-quality product. Your choice of brand and type depends more on personal preference than with any other fly-tying material. Most tiers prefer pre-waxed thread, but some like brands that have less wax and others like unwaxed thread. Some tiers prefer thread with very low stretch, while others prefer a certain elasticity. Many tiers choose thread based on color and so stick with brands that have the shades they use most often. Survey ten professional tiers about the threads they like best and you'll get five or six different answers. Danville, Uni-Thread, Gudebrod, Bennechi, and Wapsi will likely show up on any such poll.

5

Stock 6/0 (70 denier) thread in the colors you'll use most. Top row, from left: black, gray, white, olive. Bottom row: red, claret, brown, yellow.

Size Nomenclature

Thread diameter has traditionally been expressed using the "ought" system, with 3/0, 6/0, and 8/0 being the most common sizes. As in fly sizes, the larger the number, the smaller the thread. Thus, 6/0, a medium-diameter thread, is the standard for tying trout and bass flies in small and medium sizes, whereas 8/0 is a finer thread for small flies, and 3/0 for larger patterns that require tensioning coarse hair.

The ought system has been a source of confusion, however, for it turns out that when actually measured, thread labeled this way varies significantly in diameter depending on the manufacturer. In an effort to be more precise and to standardize sizing across brands, Wapsi, a leading supplier of fly-tying supplies, has led the way in labeling thread by denier, a unit of measurement used in the textile industry. Danville 6/0, for example, is 70 denier.

What Size Thread?

We used Danville 6/0 nylon (70 denier) for the patterns in this book, and it may be the only size and type of thread you'll ever need. Some tiers prefer 8/0 because it allows them to make more wraps with less build-up and thus create neater bodies and heads, especially on smaller flies. The increased number of wraps also makes the fly a bit more durable. One drawback of finer thread is that it breaks under less tension, so if you choose to use 8/0 thread, be prepared to break some thread while getting used to it.

Colors

The colors of thread most often prescribed in tying recipes are black, gray, olive, white, and tan or brown, followed by yellow, red, and claret. Keep your most-used colors loaded on separate bobbins. Also remember that color varies by manufacturer, and you may have to switch brands to get the exact shade you want. Fish are probably not as fussy about thread color as fly tiers, but then again, the exact shade of a mayfly body may indeed make a difference when trout are feeding selectively during a hatch. And in any case, advanced fly tiers are often concerned about making precise imitations as well as aesthetically pleasing creations, so finding the correct color is sometimes important.

DRY FLY HACKLE

Discussions about hackle can be confusing because the term is used to describe both the natural material—the feathers of a bird's neck—and also a part of a fly—the fibers that stick out when the hackle stem is wound around the body of a fly or a wingpost. Most discussion about hackle concerns dry fly hackle because it is generally the most expensive natural material and the one that demands the most scrutiny. The best dry fly hackle, called "genetic hackle," comes from domestic roosters bred specifically for this purpose. Tying with inferior hackle is a chore, and the results are neither pretty nor effective, whereas excellent hackle not only makes the process easier but the fly itself more pleasing and effective on the water. For one thing, it will float higher and longer.

Features of high-grade dry fly hackle:
- Stiff barbs, for flotation
- High sheen
- Barbs of uniform length on both sides of the stem
- Little or no web (the soft barbules closest to the stem)
- Slender, flexible stem (stiff stems are hard to wind)

When you inspect a whole neck (a.k.a. "cape"), also look for a high barb count throughout the sweet spot, the area of the neck that contains the hackles in the size you use most. Also check for consistent color throughout the neck. There will undoubtedly be some variation, but the sweet spot, especially, should provide hackles of consistent color throughout.

Neck or Saddle?

A neck typically is the better choice if you are tying flies in several sizes, as it contains several different feather sizes. One of the criteria for grading necks is the number of feathers in smaller sizes it contains. Premium necks yield many barbs for flies 16, 18, and down. A saddle tends to have more feathers of the same size and they tend to be larger, so if you tie a lot of flies in size 14 or 12, for example, a saddle is a good buy.

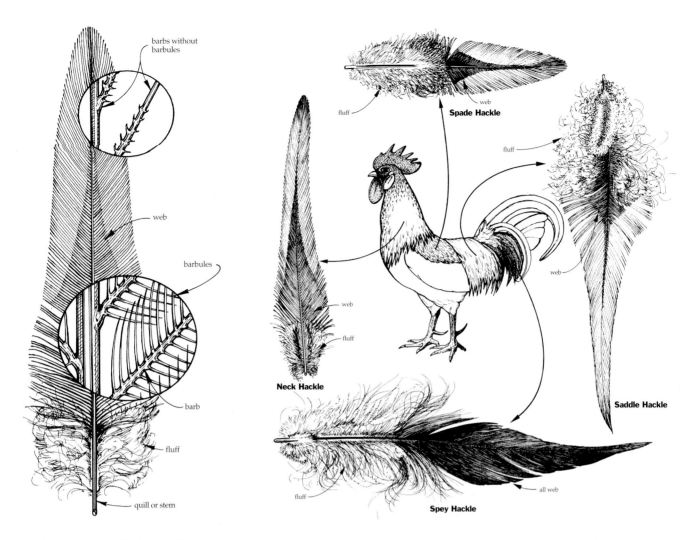

Premium dry fly hackle has stiff barbs of consistent length and color on either side of the stem, and little or no web—the soft fibers along the stem. By contrast, wet fly hackle should be "webby" so it sinks.

Hackle feathers vary in characteristics depending on their location on the bird.

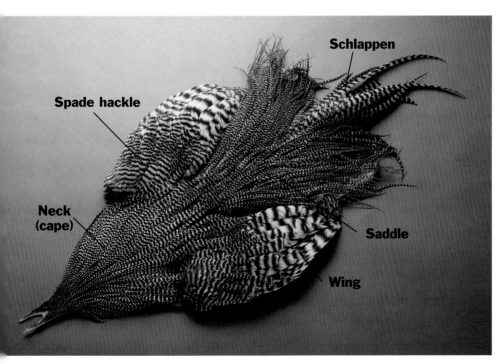

An entire rooster skin, showing the location of various types of hackle feathers. The best dry fly hackle is from the neck or saddle. Spade hackle is excellent for tails. Schlappen hackle is very webby and so is good for hackling Woolly Buggers or other underwater flies.

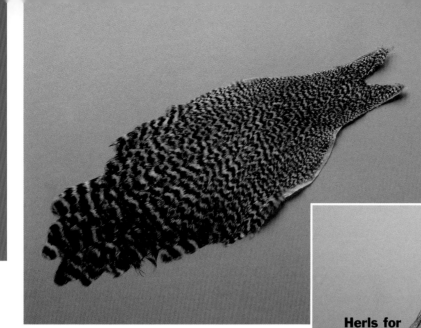

The barbs of hen neck feathers (left) are webby and not as stiff as those from rooster necks and are therefore used for wet fly hackle. Because of their small, rounded tips, hen-neck barbs are also an excellent source for hackle-tip wings in dry flies, such as the traditional Adams.

Herls for small flies

Herls for medium flies

Herls for large flies

Wherever peacock (right) is used, from nymphs like the Copper John to attractor dry flies like the Royal Wulff, its unique sparkle seems to add appeal. When selecting herls (barbs) for various size flies, note that the larger ones are found toward the middle of the feather and smaller ones toward the tip.

Colors

Necks and saddles are sold in a variety of colors, both natural and dyed. Serious tiers keep a stock on hand and are constantly on the lookout for high-grade material, especially at shops and shows where they can inspect it in person. It's a good idea to stock necks and saddles in the most-used colors—grizzly, dun, ginger, and brown—and to buy other colors as the need arises.

WING MATERIAL

You can divide the many different materials used for wings on dry flies and wet flies into three general categories: feathers, hair, and synthetics. The flies in this book have wings from all three categories.

Considering material in terms of the parts of a fly and their functions, it becomes apparent why wing material requires different qualities than hackle material. Though the hackle of a dry fly is supposed to represent the insect's legs, its structural function is to keep the fly afloat. Hence, you'll need stiff barbs with flexible stems, and material that can be wound around the body and will prop the fly up on the water. The primary function of wings, by contrast, is visual: they need to be a realistic shape and color. In his book *A Modern Dry-Fly Code*, one of the most influential books on fly architecture, Vince Marinaro lays out his conviction that the size and shape of the wings on mayfly dun imitations was the key trigger for trout feeding selectively during a hatch.

Hackle-Tip Wings

Many dry flies, including the Adams (the traditional tie, not the parachute version in this book) and the Olive Dun Quill (page 51) have wings made from hackle tips. Hen neck is the best source of such hackle, especially for flies size 16 and smaller, because its barbs are slightly wider and shorter and also have more web than those on a rooster neck; it can therefore more realistically imitate the shape of a mayfly dun wing. Thus, you're looking for almost exactly the opposite characteristics in a hen neck than you are in a rooster neck.

Hen necks are also a good source for wet fly wings, an application where the soft, water-absorbent web is not a detriment but an advantage.

OTHER FEATHERS

Peacock

Peacock is an irreplaceable natural tying material because of its iridescent blue-green flash and the way its look changes according to the angle from which it is viewed. To appreciate this feature, rotate a peacock stem slowly and watch the colors and sheen change as it turns. The same effect must occur in the water as a peacock-dressed fly moves past a fish.

The individual strands of a peacock feather, called "herls," are used on a variety of patterns, from nymphs to dry flies.

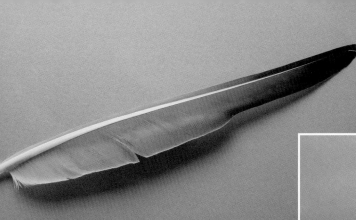

Biots are the barbs along the leading edge of a flight feather. In the goose feather above, they are the row of barbs on top. Biots are used for tails, antennae, and segmented bodies.

A whole partridge skin is more useful than individually packaged feathers, as it contains a variety of colors and sizes of feather.

Hair patches: elk (top), deer (left), and moose (right). When selecting hair, be aware that even hair of the same type varies in thickness and color. You'll want the finest deer hair you can find for very small patterns like the Serendipity. However, thicker hair is easier to spin and so is a better choice for patterns like the Muddler Minnow or Goddard Caddis that require multiple clumps of spun hair.

Preparation Tips: The tip of a peacock herl is especially fragile, though, and since the herl is normally tied in by the tip and then wound around the body of a fly, as when forming the thorax of a Copper John or the butt and shoulder of a Royal Wulff, it can break easily. One way to avoid this is by snapping off the very tip of the herl before tying it in.

Holding a peacock feather over the spout of a steaming tea kettle for a second or two will fluff up the herls and straighten out any kinky ones.

Biots

Biots are the barbs along the leading edge of a flight feather. Those from turkey and goose feathers are most commonly used in fly tying. They are used to form tails, antennae, legs, and wing cases for nymph patterns.

Preparation Tip: Longer biots are used to make segmented bodies on some dry fly patterns, but biots in general are brittle and may break when wound around a hook. Soaking them in water for two or three minutes makes them more flexible.

A feature of biots useful to the fly tier is the curved tip on the end of each barb. A pair of biots can be arranged so that the tips flare away from each other, as in the tails of a Copper John.

Partridge

It's smart to buy a whole partridge skin, rather than packaged feathers, as you will get a larger variety of colors and sizes. Likewise, you'll be able to take paired feathers from the skin for patterns that call for mated wings.

HAIR

Deer, elk, and moose hair is widely used for heads, bodies, and tails. Thickness and color of hair varies with the animal and species, so which type of hair you choose depends on both the size of the fly and the part of it you're building. For patterns that require spun deer-hair heads and bodies, such as the Muddler Minnow, Dave's Hopper, and Goddard Caddis, thicker and lighter-colored hair is easier to work with and looks

9

Animal tails, from top: calf tail, gray squirrel, red squirrel.

The rule of thumb is to use the gauge of weighting wire that matches the gauge of the hook.

Heavy .030   size 2

Medium-heavy .025   size 6

Medium .020   size 8

Fine .01   size 16

size 18

best. (One exception: On a small fly like the Serendipity, which has a spun deer-hair wing, finer hair is more appropriate.) Deer hair is darker on top because the individual hairs have black tips. To get lighter hair, take a bunch closer to the hide.

Thinner, darker hair is better for making tails and wings. Moose hair makes excellent tailing material because it is straight and fine. Elk hair is used for the wings on many caddis patterns.

Always comb out the underfur before putting a bunch of hair in your stacker; the tips will align more easily with the very short hair removed.

Calf Tail, Squirrel Tail, Bucktail

These materials are crinkly and difficult to stack as they come off the hide. Shampooing and using conditioner will make them more supple and easier to handle. In some cases, such as for the wing of a Royal Wulff tied in smaller sizes, you can substitute calf body hair for calf tail, the body hair being easier to stack and more manageable.

WEIGHTING WIRE

Lead-free weighting wire and split shots are now available to protect the environment. Weighting wire comes in a variety of gauges, from fine through heavy, the gauge you use determined by the hook size and how deep you fish the fly. As a rule of thumb, match the

gauge of weighting wire to the gauge of the hook, which can be done simply by holding one next to the other. As discussed in more detail in the introduction to chapter 2, may tiers prefer to underweight their nymphs, using wire slightly finer than the hook, so they have the option of fishing the fly off the bottom. You can always add a small split shot if needed.

Since weighting wire is an integral part of so many flies, from nymphs to streamers, you should pay attention to a few details in its application.

- After you've wrapped the wire and trimmed the waste, press the tips, forward and rear, snug against the shank with your fingernail so the body will have a smooth profile when you wrap thread or dubbing over the wire.
- Anchor the wrapped wire securely to the shank with sufficient thread wraps around it and also with thread dams at either end. Loosely anchored wire can begin to slide back and forth on the shank, pushing loose other materials and contributing to the early demise of the fly.
- When using thicker weighting wire, after you've wound it around the hook, trim the ends by pulling on them until they snap, rather than cutting them. This method will create tapered ends that sit more snugly against the hook shank and result in a smoother body when thread is wound over them.

10

2

Nymphs

Nymphs, as a group, are generally less demanding to tie than dry flies because they're compact and do not have upright wings, which require some finesse. Also, in many cases, a scraggly nymph body is acceptable or even preferable to a tidy one, as the stray wisps of dubbing and hair realistically imitate the natural's body.

The patterns in this chapter were chosen because, as a group, they represent the underwater stages of the most important insects to fly fishers—mayflies, caddisflies, and stoneflies—and are effective in waters everywhere. A freshwater crustacean, the scud/cressbug, is included to round out your underwater-fly collection.

WEIGHTING NYMPHS
Because nymph patterns imitate food forms that live on the bottom of the stream, most nymph recipes call for weighting wire. Non-lead weighting wire, also called "non-toxic," is replacing traditional lead for this purpose, as many fisheries now prohibit the use of lead in flies, lures, and sinkers.

Weighting wire is available in gauges from .010 (very fine) to .035 (heavy), and it's a good idea to stock a few sizes. Although the rule of thumb for weighting flies is to use wire approximately the same gauge as the hook, many veteran fly tiers underweight their nymphs by using wire a bit finer than the hook. An underweighted nymph is more versatile than a heavier one: it can be fished, as is, just below the surface or in the middle of the water column, yet still be taken to the bottom by adding a split shot to the leader. Also, an underweighted nymph tends to move and drift more naturally than one that is too heavily weighted, and is therefore more enticing.

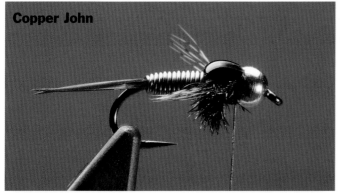
Copper John

Kaufmann's Golden Stone

Serendipity

Olive Shellback Scud

Copper John

Hook	2X long, 2X stout nymph hook, size 10–18
Thread	Black 6/0 (70 denier)
Head	Gold bead
Weight	Non-lead wire, gauge of hook or one gauge lighter.
Underbody	Thread, tapered
Tail	Brown turkey biots
Body	Medium copper wire
Wing case	Thin Skin and Flashabou
Thorax	Peacock herl
Legs	Section of partridge feather

The Copper John, created by John Barr, of Boulder, Colorado, is currently the best-selling pattern in America for the simple reason that it catches fish everywhere. It has several advantages over conventional nymphs: First, trout everywhere seem to find the metallic flash irresistible. Though the Copper John's profile suggests a mayfly nymph, the pattern is also effective when trout are feeding on caddisfly and stonefly nymphs. Another key to its success is that the copper-wound body sinks like a stone, in many cases taking the fly to the bottom without added split shot and thus achieving a very natural drift. And finally, it's a compact and durable pattern—you can catch a lot of fish on one without damaging it.

Experiments with other colors of wire on the body—especially red, silver, and blue—have proved effective. Barr's recently published *Barr Flies* (Stackpole, 2007) contains tying and fishing tips for the Copper John and its variations.

1. Pinch down the barb of the hook with pliers. This should be an automatic first step for conscientious fly tiers when using barbed hooks, and though we do not show this step in the patterns that follow, we hope you'll do it each time.

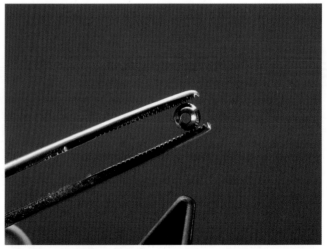

2. The hole through a fly-tying bead is smaller on one side . . . .

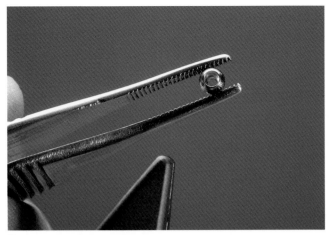

3. . . .than on the other, so you can easily thread the bead around the bend of a hook.

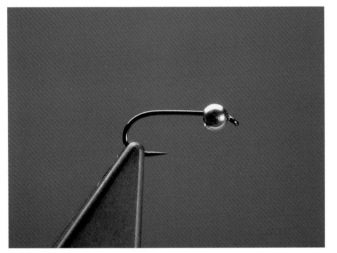

4. Place the point of the hook through the *smaller* hole of the bead, and push the bead around the bend and forward to the eye.

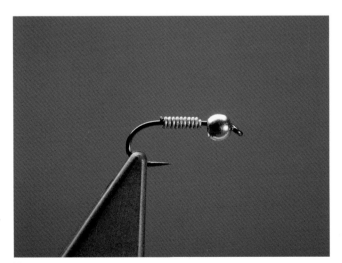

5. Wind a length of weighting wire tightly around half the length of the hook shaft, trim both ends, and push the tips of each end snugly against the shaft with your thumbnail.

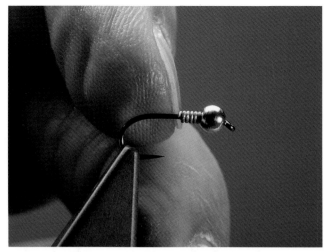

6. Push the wire forward until the forward end tucks into the hole in the bead.

7. The weighting wire in place.

8. A strip of turkey-feather biots.

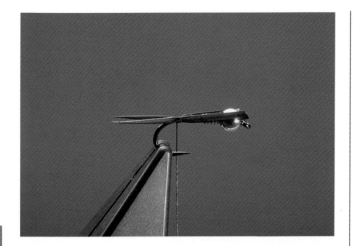

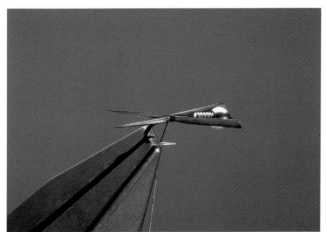

9. Clip two barbs from the biot stem and tie them in at the bend, positioned so the barbs bend away from each other in a V.

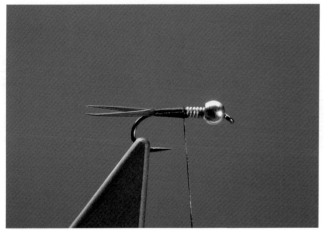

10. Trim the waste ends off the tails and wind the thread forward snugly over the biot stubs to form a tapered base for the body.

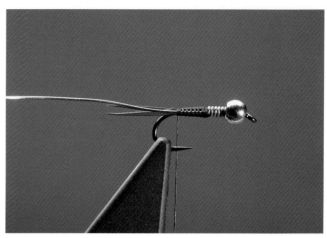

11. Tie in a length of copper wire, a few inches long, by placing one end up against the rear end of the weighting wire and holding the copper wire *along the side of the hook,* not on the top or bottom. This position creates a more realistic nymph profile.

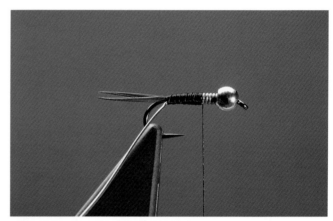

12. Wrap thread back and forth over this copper wire base to securely anchor it to the hook shaft.

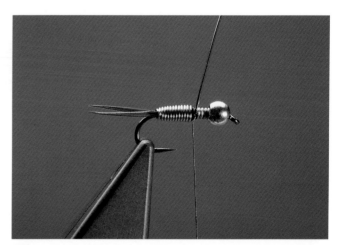

13. Let the bobbin hang. To form the body, wrap the remaining copper wire forward to where you tied it in, making each wrap snugly against the previous one. Trim the waste, and press the tip snugly against the shank with your thumbnail.

Tool Tip

Use your heavier scissors for trimming copper wire so as not to dull your tying scissors.

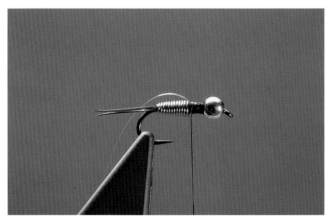

14. Tie in a length of Flashabou just in front of the copper wire, where shown, and let the strand hang rearward, out of the way.

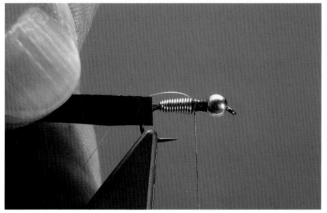

15. Cut a strip of Thin Skin the width of the hook gap.

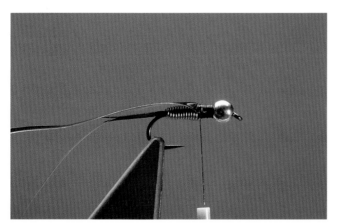

16. Tie in the Thin Skin in front of the copper wire, shiny side up (i.e., the side from which you removed the paper backing).

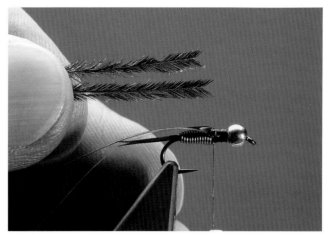

17. Select two peacock herls for the thorax.

Material Tip

Remember to break off the very tip of a peacock herl before you tie it in. (See page 9.)

18. Tie in the herls behind the bead.

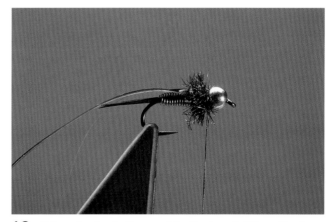

19. Wrap the herls forward to the bead. Wrap firmly and evenly, but not so tightly that the feathers break. It may take some trial and error to find the breaking point of peacock.

20. Select a partridge feather from which to make legs for the nymph.

21. Strip the fluff from the base of the feather.

22. Pull off two small bundles of barbs. Tie in one bundle on the near side of the hook, where shown, and the other on the far side.

Technique Tip

Don't wrap these bundles tightly yet; just make a few wraps and let the weight of the hanging bobbin hold them in place. You can then pull the legs forward or aft into the correct position.

23. To get the legs the right length, pull the two bundles forward (to the right, in the photo) one at a time, until the tips are directly above the point of the hook. When both bundles are in the right position, tie them down.

24. The finished legs.

25. Flip the Thin Skin forward, over the herl; tie it down in front of the bead, and trim the waste.

26. Flip the Flashabou strip forward over the herl, tie it down in front of the bead, and trim the waste.

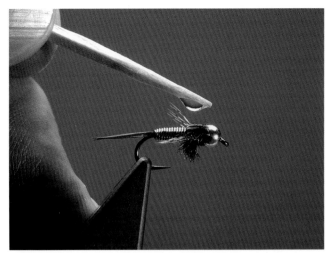

27. Apply a drop of epoxy to the head.

28. The completed Copper John. It takes some practice to create an evenly segmented body and a neatly finished wing case, thorax and legs, but remember that there are endless variations of this pattern, and you may discover some yourself in the process of learning to tie it.

Nymphs

Hook	Curved caddis or scud hook, size 14–22
Thread	Claret 6/0 (70 denier)
Body	Claret Z-lon
Head	Spun and clipped deer hair (the finer the better)

The Serendipity was created by Madison River guide Ross Marigold to imitate midge pupae, and has since become a go-to pattern for guides and fly fishers everywhere.

Serendipities are simple to tie and require few materials. They are most commonly tied in claret, black, olive, and gray, the range of colors of most midge pupae, and therefore the color of thread and Z-lon you use for this pattern will vary accordingly.

The segmented body is one of the keys to this imitation, so you must take care with how you wind the Z-lon body to create this effect (steps 2 and 3, below).

Serendipities are usually fished on the bottom in streams and rivers, where the fish take them for pupae. But as Dave Hughes points out in *Trout Flies* (Stackpole Books, 1999), the pattern can be adapted to float in the middle of the water column or just under the surface, to imitate emerging nymphs. If you intend to fish a Serendipity this way, don't clip the deer hair short, as shown in the final step below. Instead, leave it long to imitate the nymph's wings and body emerging from its pupal form. If you want the fly to drift in the film, coat the unclipped wing with floatant.

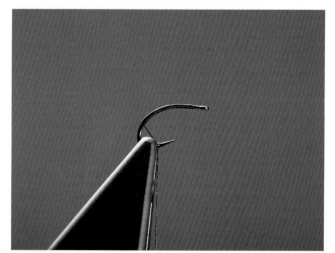

1. Start the thread just behind the eye of the hook and wind rearward into the bend, stopping where shown.

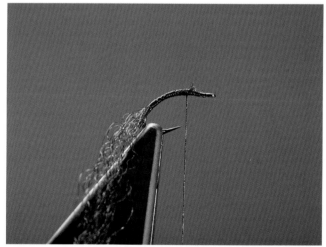

2. Tie in a strand of Z-lon at the bend, and then wind the thread forward, stopping ¼ hook-length from the eye.

Material Tip

Z-lon is a braided bundle of crinkly synthetic fibers, and as it comes from the package, it may be too thick for making bodies of small flies. You want a bundle that, when twisted, is about the diameter of the hook shank. So, before putting a piece of Z-lon on the hook, twist it, and if it looks too thick, pull out a few fibers until it's the right diameter.

3. Twist the Z-lon into a tight strand and wind it forward, pausing to retwist the bundle as you wind if you feel it loosening.

Technique Tip

Patterns with segmented bodies, like this one, require snug, closely abutting wraps with clearly articulated seams between them. The segmented effect is lost if the Z-lon—or whatever material you're using—unwinds into a loose bundle. So keep it twisted, and wrap it with constant tension.

4. Clean and stack a small bundle of fine deer hair.

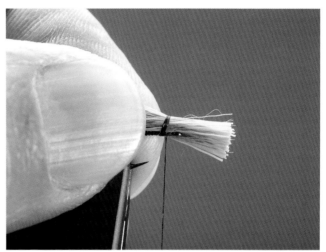

5. Hold the middle of the bundle over the hook, just behind the eye, and make two soft loops around it and the hook.

6. Gripping the rear (left) half of the deer-hair bundle between thumb and forefinger, pull down on the thread and at the same time release your grip on the bundle. The deer hair will flare around the hook, as shown. Take two more turns of thread through the spun deer hair, just behind the eye, and whip finish.

7. The forward section of the spun deer hair will become the head, and the rear section the wing. Begin forming the head by trimming the forward hairs into shorter lengths.

8. Trim the forward hairs into a cube.

9. Continue trimming the head into a sphere.

10. Finally, gather the wing portion of the deer hair with your left hand and trim it to length. Serendipity.

Hook	6X long, size 2-10
Weighting wire	
	Non-lead, diameter of hook shank
Thread	Brown 6/0 (70 denier)
Antennae	Ginger turkey biots
Tail	Turkey biots
Rib	Vinyl ribbing material, such as Swannundaze
Abdomen	Kaufmann's Golden Stone Blend, or brown nymph dubbing
Wing case	Turkey tail feather, three sections
Thorax	Same as abdomen
Head	Same as abdomen

Created by Randall Kaufmann, this is the standard pattern for nymphs of both the salmon fly and the golden stonefly, large insects found primarily on rivers of the western United States.

Stonefly nymphs are most effective when fished right on the bottom, as stoneflies spend their entire lives there. They even emerge by crawling to shore, rather than floating to the surface and becoming airborne, like mayflies and caddisflies. Therefore, weighting this pattern is a necessity, either by wrapping weighting wire around the shank or by adding a split shot to your leader.

A Kaufmann Blend (in this case, the Kaufmann's Golden Stone Blend) is a good choice for dubbing the abdomen of this fly. Each Kaufmann Blend contains several shades of fur, resulting in a look that's proven very effective, but one that's hard to duplicate on your own unless you stock many colors of fur and are willing to experiment.

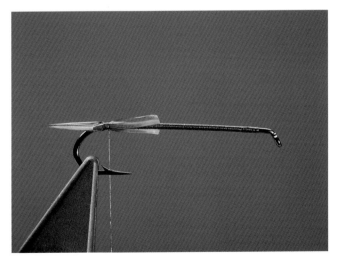

1. Having tied in thread behind the eye and wound rearward to the bend, install the tails by tying in two ginger biots at the bend, positioned so they curve away from each other.

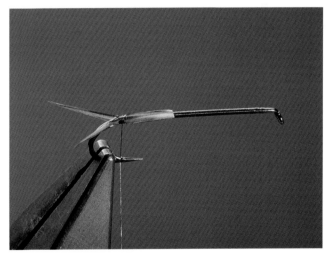

2. The tails tied in.

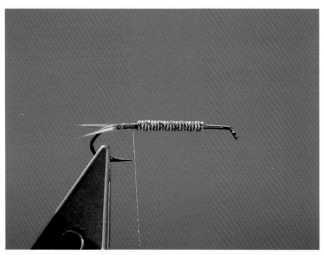

3. Optional: Wrap weighting wire around one-half of the hook shank.

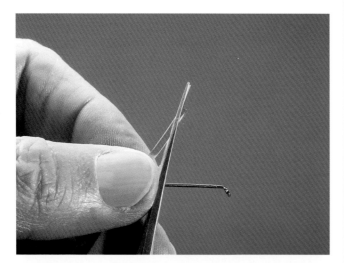

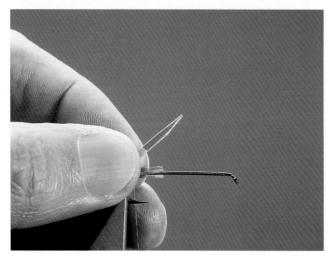

4. Cut one end of a 6-inch piece of vinyl ribbing at an angle.

5. Tie in the cut end of the vinyl ribbing at the bend.

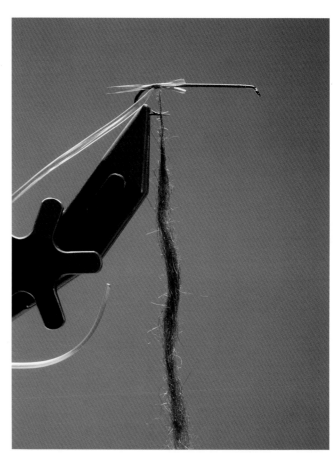

6. Twist a length of dubbing onto the thread.

7. Wind the dubbing forward two-thirds of the shank, twisting the strand as you go to keep it tight.

8. Wind the vinyl ribbing forward over the dubbing, trim the waste, and tie off.

9. To begin the wing case, select a section of turkey feather one hook-gap wide.

10. To make a V-notch in the end, first fold the turkey feather in half.

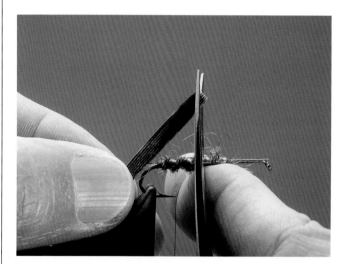

11. Cut the end of the feather at a 45-degree angle.

12. Unfold the feather, and you have your V-notch. Prepare two more turkey-feather sections in the same way so you have three wing cases.

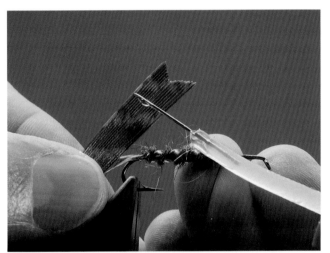

13. Apply flexible cement (or artist's fixative) to the prepared feathers to prevent them from splitting.

14. Tie in the first wing case with the V-notch facing rearward, and trim the waste.

15. Apply more dubbing to the working thread, wrap it forward over the feather butt.

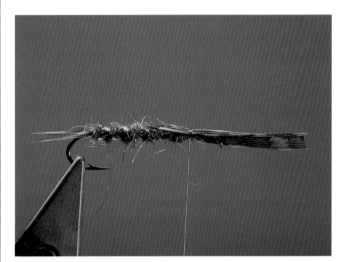

16. Tie in the second wing case just in front of the first, and trim the waste.

17. Add a length of dubbing to the working thread, wind over the feather butt of the second wing case.

18. Tie in the third wing case and repeat step 17.

19. Tie in a pair of biots for antennae.

20. The completed Kaufmann's Golden Stone. This pattern won't win any beauty contests, but neither will a real stonefly nymph. The point is that the fly catches a lot of big trout.

Overhead view, showing angle of biots.

Hook	1X or 2X long, size 12–18
Weight	Non-lead wire (optional)
Thread	Olive 6/0 (70 denier)
Tail	Olive hackle
Shellback	Clear plastic strip (plastic freezer bag, or commercial scud-back)
Rib	Working thread
Body	Olive dubbing

Scuds (freshwater shrimp) and cressbugs (so named because they're found in watercress, but also known as sow-bugs) are freshwater crustaceans found in aquatic vegetation in slower stretches of moving water and in ponds and lakes. They are a significant food source for trout, as they are available all year long, unlike aquatic insects that hatch and disappear. And although trout may ignore scuds and cressbugs when a hatch is on, any water with aquatic weeds, such as watercress or elodea, will support a population of scuds and/or cressbugs, and the trout will take them. When fishing water known to contain scuds or cressbugs, watch for trout nosing around in the weeds. Cast the fly just upstream of the feeding fish and let it dead-drift in front of them.

Some scud recipes call for scud hooks with curved shanks, because this crustacean curls up when at rest. However, scuds straighten out when they swim, and so many tiers prefer to tie the pattern on a straight hook, as it is fished as if swimming, either drifting with the current in a stream or retrieved slowly in still water.

The only difference between the scud and alternate cressbug pattern shown here is the underside of the fly. For the scud, dubbing fibers are picked out and left sticking down to represent legs. For the cressbug, the fibers are left sticking out the sides, and the bottom is trimmed flat.

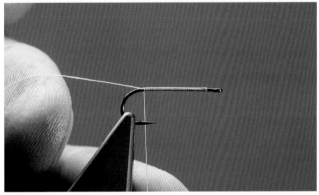

1. Start thread at the bend, leaving a 3-inch tag hanging out the back, and then wind forward and back to build a thread base. (If you wish to weight the fly, wind weighting wire around the shank now.)

2. Select an olive hackle feather.

Nymphs

3. Pull off a section of barbs and tie it in at the bend. The tail should be about ½ shank-length long. Trim the butts and wind thread over them.

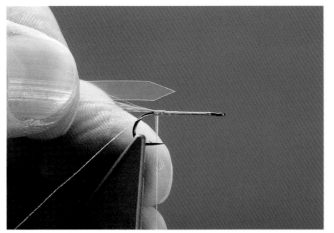

4. Cut a plastic strip about ⅛-inch wide (width will vary with size of fly), and trim one end to a point to reduce bulk at the tie-in point.

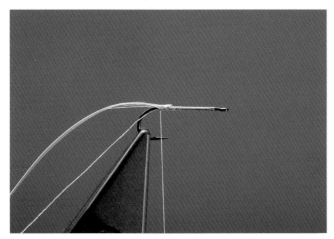

5. Tie in the pointed end of the strip at the bend and let the rest of the strip hang off the back of the hook.

6. Advance the thread to the midpoint of the hook and twist on a length of dubbing, leaving about ½ inch of bare thread at the top.

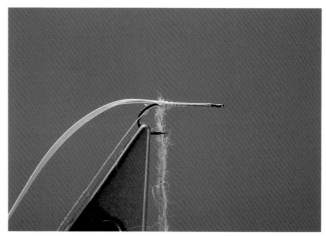

7. Wind thread back to the bend.

8. Wind the dubbing forward, stopping one eye-length behind the eye (to leave room for tying down the plastic when you fold it forward), and make a few wraps to tie it down.

9. Flip the plastic strip forward and tie it down just behind the eye. Trim the waste.

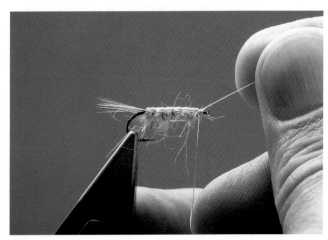

10. Take the tag end of thread hanging from the rear and wind it forward around the body in widely spaced wraps to form the rib. Whip finish and trim the end of the thread.

11. If you're making a scud, use a dubbing needle or bodkin to pull strands of dubbing from the bottom of the body out from underneath the ribbing, to represent legs.

12. Shellback Scud.

13. To create a cressbug, simply pull dubbing strands from the sides, rather than the bottom . . .

14. . . . and then trim the bottom flat.

15. Rear view of cressbug trimming.

16. The finished Cressbug. Compare this to the finished Shellback Scud (Step 12) and you can see the significant difference in profile. Collecting samples from weedy areas of ponds, lakes, or slower stretches of streams will indicate which pattern to use.

3

Wet Flies and Emergers

Wet flies and emergers represent aquatic insects on the way up or down; that is, insects in the process of emerging from nymph to dun, or duns that have fallen back into the water and drowned. At certain stages of a hatch, this type of fly will catch trout when a dry fly or nymph will not, because the fish are keying on these helpless forms. But at the same time, there may also be duns floating on the surface, so the situation can be confusing; fish are rising everywhere, but they're not hitting duns. And in most cases, discovering the right fly type is a matter of trial-and-error. When fish are rising but not taking drys, try an emerger.

Trout don't seem as discriminating about subsurface insects as they are about those on the surface, which they have the time and lighting to scrutinize. Therefore, most emerger and wet fly patterns are impressionistic. They need not be detailed replicas of a particular insect, as long as they're the right size and color. It's probably the undulating action of the wet fly more than its form that attracts the fish.

Partridge and Yellow Soft-Hackled Wet Fly

CDC Emerger

Klinkhamer

Hook	Standard wet fly, size 10–16
Thread	Pearsall's gossamer silk, yellow
Hackle	Gray partridge

Soft-hackled wet flies may have been the first artificial flies ever tied. A dozen patterns appear in *A Treatise on Fishing with a Hook* by Dame Juliana Berners, published in 1496, and from the beginning of the sport, this pattern type was used for European brown trout. But wet flies were largely ignored in America until their rediscovery in the mid-twentieth century by such tiers such as Jim Leisenring, author of *The Art of Tying the Wet Fly* (Crown, 1971), and Sylvester Nemes, author of *The Soft-Hackled Fly* (Stackpole Books, 1975) and *The Soft-Hackled Fly Addict* (Stackpole Books, 1993).

Soft-hackle patterns represent drowned mayflies. The soft, webby hackle from partridge or hen chicken is ideal for such patterns because it lets the fly sink and also undulates in the water. When buying partridge, it's best to get a whole skin, rather than packaged feathers, as the skin will contain more shades and sizes of feather.

Recipe notes: Some tiers add a thorax of hare's mask to this pattern. This addition is not necessary for an effective pattern, though it does no harm. Also, the use of Pearsall's silk thread, instead of nylon, is significant. When Pearsall's gossamer yellow gets wet, it turns just the right shade of olive for this pattern.

1. Start thread at the eye and wind to the bend.

2. Build a thread base by winding the thread forward, covering the first layer in close, even turns. Stop one eye-length from the eye.

Wet Flies and Emergers

31

3. Select a light gray partridge feather for hackle.

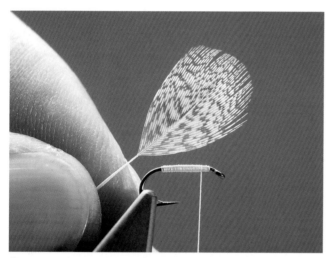

4. Strip the fluff from the base of the stem.

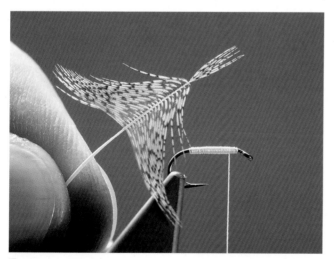

5. Stroke a section of barbs toward the base, so the feather looks like this.

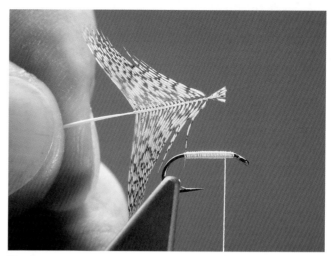

6. Snip the tip of the feather off with your scissors to form a triangular head.

7. This is the tie-in point of the prepared hackle feather.

8. Tie in the prepared hackle behind the eye.

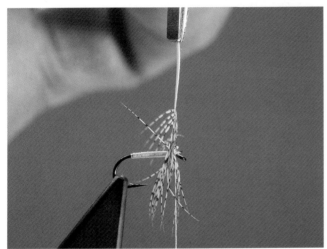

10. The finished Partridge and Yellow Soft-Hackled Wet Fly. If you tie a lot of dry flies, this pattern may look bereft of hackle, but the sparseness is the key.

9. Grasping the tip of the feather with hackle pliers, wind the hackle around the hook two times. Remember that the hackle must be sparse because the fly is fished wet. Too much hackle will make it float.

Hook	1X short caddis hook, size 14–20
Thread	Brown 6/0 (70 denier)
Tail	Brown Z-lon
Body	Brown turkey biot
Thorax	Superfine PMD dubbing
Wing	CDC, nipple plume (a.k.a. oiler puff)

CDC stands for Cul de Canard (French for "duck's bum"), a term coined by Henri Bresson in the late 1950s for the small, oil-impregnated feathers surrounding a duck's preen glands. CDC feathers are naturally waterproof, not only because of their oil, but also because of their barb structure, as Dutch tier Hans Weilenmann has pointed out. For this reason, never dress CDC feathers with floatant: it will make them sink. The most significant feature of CDC to the fisherman is that the feathers are fluffy and lightweight, with filaments that undulate seductively with even the slightest trace of air or current. It is this lifelike movement that makes them such a unique and valuable fly-tying material. For more on the history and use of CDC feathers, see *Tying Flies with CDC,* by Leon Links (Stackpole Books, 2002).

CDC feathers vary in structure and size, depending on where they are located relative to the preen gland and also according to the size and type of bird. This recipe calls for a nipple plume, sometimes called an oiler puff, the small feather that covers the preen gland. Here, this feather imitates the new and sometimes tangled wing of a dun struggling to escape the surface film.

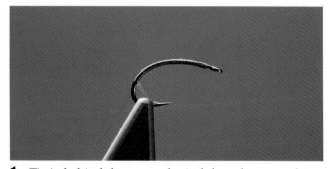

1. Tie in behind the eye and wind thread rearward to the bend.

Technique Tip

Flattened thread creates a smoother and less bulky base over which to wind bodies. Most fly-tying thread is twisted as it comes off the spool. It can be flattened by spinning the bobbin counterclockwise.

2. Tie in a sparse bundle of Z-lon at the bend for a tail.

3. Trim the end of the tail so it's about 1½ hook-gap long.

4. Trim the waste end of the tail.

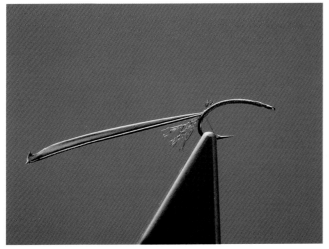

5. Pull, don't cut, a biot off the stem so the barb has a notch at the end. Tie the biot in at the bend, by its tip, with the notch up.

6. Grasp the butt of the biot with hackle pliers and wind it forward to form the segmented body. Wind gently—biots are brittle. Note: The slim profile of this body illustrates the advantages of winding over a base of flattened thread.

Material Tip

If you come across a recipe that calls for a smooth body made from a biot, tie the biot in with the notch down.

7. Tie in a CDC nipple plume with a few wraps just behind the eye with the tips pointed toward the eye (opposite orientation of most wings).

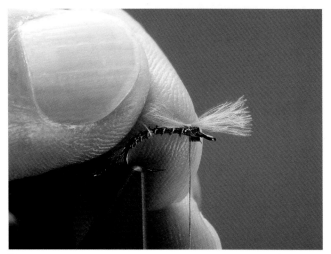

8. Grasp the butts of the CDC with your fingers (or tweezers) and pull the wing rearward until it extends about one hook-gap beyond the tie-in point. Make a few more wraps to secure the wing in this position, and trim the butts.

10. Wind the dubbing forward to the wing, hold it in a vertical position, and make two wraps of dubbing in front of it. Whip finish to complete the CDC Emerger.

The segmented body is a significant feature on this sparsely dressed pattern, as is the fluffy CDC wing, which will undulate seductively, even when the fly is at rest in still water.

9. With the thread hanging a bit to the rear of the wing (leaving space for a few winds of dubbing), pull the bobbin down and apply some extra-fine dubbing to the thread.

Hook	Klinkhamer Extreme, Partridge 15BNX, or curved scud hook, size 12–20
Thread	Gray 6/0 (70 denier)
Wingpost	White poly yarn
Hackle	Dun
Body	Tan dubbing
Thorax	Peacock herl

This unusual parachute pattern was created by Dutch tier Hans van Klinken in 1984 while fishing for grayling during caddis hatches on the Glomma River in Norway. Its inspiration was a large, caseless caddis larva he found in the stomach of a grayling. Van Klinken tied the pattern on a large Partridge grub hook and made a few extra turns of hackle, parachute style, to ensure that the big fly wouldn't sink. It turned out to be a deadly design. The long, curved hook let the body of the fly sink farther beneath the surface than smaller emerger patterns tied on conventional hooks, yet the parachute hackle kept the head of the fly on the surface. Van Klinken's prototype had a thorax of polypropylene dubbing, but a switch to peacock herl brought much better results.

Since its introduction in Scandinavia, the Klinkhamer has become popular around the world. It is effective during caddis hatches on broken water, but in smaller sizes, imitates a midge pupa hanging in the film.

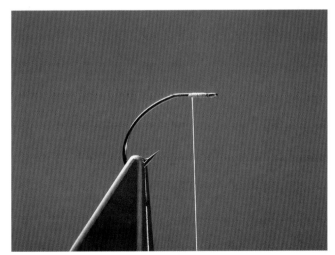

1. Start thread behind the eye and wind it halfway down the straight part of the shank.

Note the odd shape of this Klinkhamer Extreme hook by Partridge. If you can't find this hook, you can approximate its shape by straightening the forward third of a long-shank nymph hook.

2. For the wingpost, tie in a 2-inch length of white poly yarn where the thread is hanging.

Wet Flies and Emergers

3. Prepare a dun hackle feather by trimming off the butt end until the remaining piece is no more than 25 percent web.

4. Trim the barbs off the base of the stem on both sides, as shown, to create a tie-in point.

5. Tie in the hackle where you tied in the wingpost.

6. Lift both wingpost and hackle with one hand, and with the other, wind thread around the base of the wing and hackle.

38

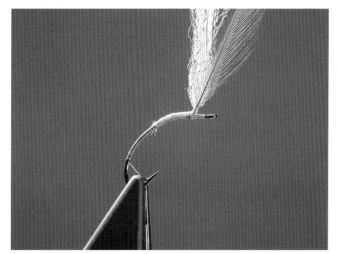

7. Trim the waste end of the poly yarn wing with a tapered cut, so the body will be smooth when dubbing is wound over the stub.

8. Wind the thread rearward, over the butts of poly yarn, and stop at the far end of the bend. Pull some thread from the bobbin, let it hang, and apply dubbing.

9. Wind the dubbing forward. Stop where the hook shank begins to straighten, before the wingpost, so you leave room to wind the peacock herl.

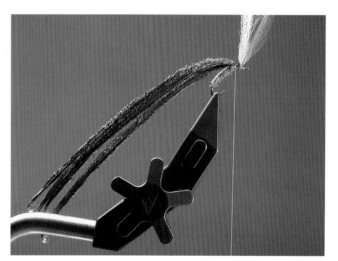

10. Tie in three of four peacock herls by their tips where the thread is hanging. Remember to break off the very tips of the herls before tying them in.

11. Twist the herls gently into one strand.

12. Wind the herl strand a few turns behind, then a few turns in front of the wingpost to form the thorax.

13. Trim the waste from the herl strand and secure the thread with two half hitches.

14. Reposition the hook in the vise so the hook points down.

15. Wind hackle with the good side (i.e., the shiny side) of the feather toward the eye (to the right, in the photo).

16. Tie off the hackle.

17. Trim waste from top of hackle.

18. Throw a whip finish on the wingpost, on top of the hackle, and trim the thread waste.

Technique Tip

(from Dick Talleur's *Guide to Fly Tying*)

Throwing a whip finish on a parachute wingpost, especially on small flies, is easier for some tiers with a Matarelli-type whip-finish tool than by hand.

19. Reposition the fly in the vise, as shown, and trim the wingpost to about twice the length of the hook gap. (There is no hard and fast rule for the height of the wingpost. Some tiers prefer shorter versions than this.)

Technique Tip

Always apply a drop of flexible cement to the base of the wingpost in parachute patterns to prevent the hackle from riding up the wingpost.

20. The finished Klinkhamer. You'll see several variations of this odd-looking pattern in shops and catalogs, as it is tied in a wide range of sizes and colors to imitate regional hatches. The distinctive features in all, however, are the curved body and prominent wingpost, which create the "hanging parachute" profile.

4

Dry Flies

Dry fly fishing is the apex of the sport. That's not meant to be snobbish. Catching fish with a dry fly is just more fun than any other way. But it also requires more skill, both at tying the flies and presenting them. It's true that trout see more subsurface food forms, including insect pupae and larvae, baitfish, and crustaceans, than they do floating insects, and that most of the time, on most waters, you'll catch more fish with subsurface flies than with drys. But casting a dry fly to a rising fish is simply more engaging than drifting a nymph or wet fly because you see all the action—the rise, the touch-down of the fly, the drift, the take. Likewise, the dun phase of an aquatic insect is generally more interesting and inspiring to tiers than the underwater phases. Thus, a disproportionate amount of ink has been spent on dry fly fishing and tying.

A few points distinguish the tying of dry flies from the tying of other types. First, the requirement that the fly must float dictates the use of specific materials: lightweight hooks, high-quality hackle, buoyant body material. Also, tying dry flies means more attention to wings. In traditional Catskill patterns, the wings are upright and divided, a technique that takes some practice to master, and some caddis patterns, like the Henryville Special, have a tricky wing construction. Though the wing in a parachute pattern is reduced to a single vertical post, constructing this feature and winding hackle around it takes some practice.

Finally, dry fly patterns—especially those that represent specific insects—need to be more carefully built than underwater patterns, with just the right amount and color of materials and the right profile to attract trout when they're feeding selectively.

Trico

Goddard Caddis

Royal Wulff

Rusty CDC Biot Spinner

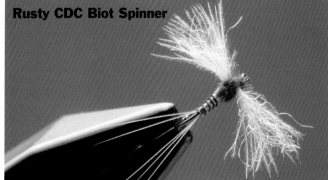

Amayfly that has emerged from the stream bottom and shed its nymphal shuck is known as a dun. Mayfly duns float on the water for a minute or so until their wings are dry and then fly to streamside vegetation, where they molt a final time to become spinners. During a hatch, mayfly duns are prime targets for trout, and this phase of the insect is the inspiration for the classic dry fly, with its distinctive upright wings and long tail.

Light Cahill   Difficulty: Moderate

Hook	Standard dry fly, size 12–20
Thread	Tan 6/0 (70 denier)
Tail	Light ginger hackle fibers
Wings	Lemon barred wood duck flank fibers
Body	Cream dubbing
Hackle	Light ginger

The Light Cahill is an example of the classic Catskill dry fly, a style created to imitate mayfly duns on the fast, broken water of northeastern streams. Catskill drys have prominent, upright wings, slender bodies and tails, and hackle wound as a collar, a basic style seen in the Adams, Hendrickson, Blue-Winged Olive, Trico, and March Brown, and many others. Learn to tie one pattern, and you can tie any of them simply by substituting materials. The key feature of a Catskill dry fly's architecture is its "footprint": It sits up on its hackle collar and tail, so it rides high on rough water and stays visible to the angler. This footprint also is thought to be a trigger for feeding trout: from below, a Catskill dry apparently resembles the way a newly hatched mayfly dun sits on the water—at least on broken water. On flat water, other styles, such as parachutes, Compara-duns, and no-hackles, which sit farther down in the film, are more realistic and often more effective.

The Light Cahill was chosen for this collection because it is one of the most versatile Catskill patterns, taking fish during the various hatches of sulfurs in the East and pale morning duns and pale evening duns in the West. In fact, whenever you see light-tan mayflies in the air, a Light Cahill is a good bet. As always, matching the size of the hatch is crucial, so as a starter, tie these in size 14, 16, and 18.

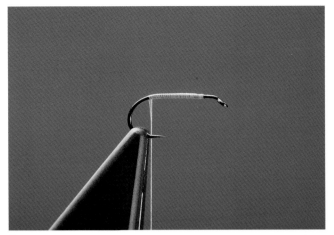

1. Tie in at the front of the hook and wind rearward to the bend.

2. Barbs from this part of a spade feather (found on the edge of a cape) make the best tail material because they have long, stiff barbs with little or no web.

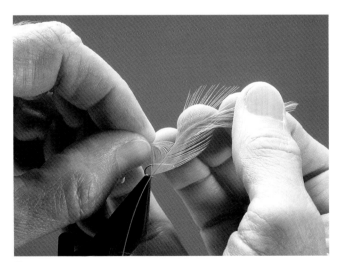

3. Remove a bundle of barbs by grasping their tips (left hand, above) and pulling the feather the other way. Doing the opposite—pulling the barbs away from the feather—will pull the tips out of alignment.

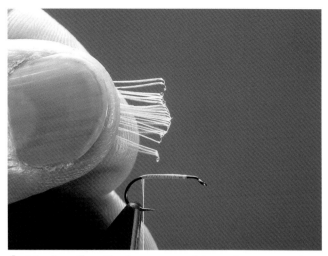

4. The bundle of barbs, removed from the stem and ready to tie in to make the tail.

5. Tie in the tail at the bend, positioned so that it's one hook-shank long.

Technique Tip

Eyeball the tail length before cinching it down. If it's short or long, you can always slide it forward or backward before securing it to the hook.

Dry Flies

45

6. Trim the tail butts as shown.

7. Wind forward over the tail butts, stopping ⅓ shank-length from the eye.

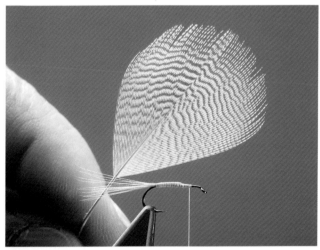

8. Begin prepping the wing by stripping the fluff from the stem of a lemon-barred wood duck feather.

9. Hold the feather against the hook to find the right length barbs for the wing, and stroke the tips forward so they're even.

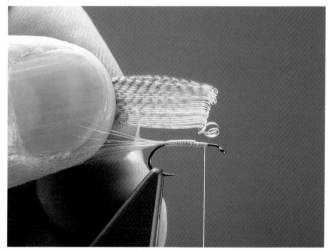

10. Pull a bundle of barbs from one side of the stem, using the technique from step 3.

Technique Tip

You will need to set this bundle of barbs down while you get a second bundle. If you set it on your knee, rather than on the tying bench, it will be less likely to blow away and also much easier to pick up.

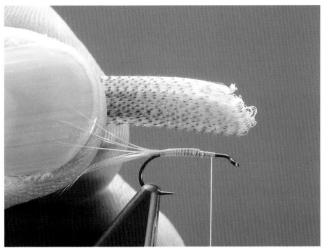

11. Pull a second bundle of barbs from the other side of the stem. Now you have material for two wings with tips aligned.

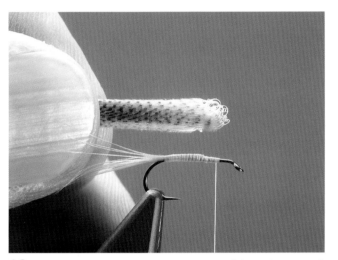

12. Stack the two wings, one on top of the other, good side up, and fold them in half once, and then again.

13. Tie in the folded wing bundle where the thread is hanging, tips toward the eye.

14. Trim the butts at an angle.

15. Pull half the clump of wings rearward.

47

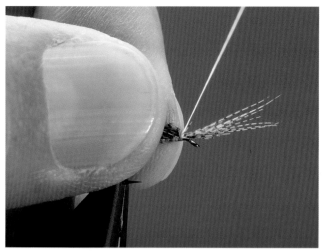

16. Make a turn of thread through the gap.

17. Wind thread behind the wing.

18. Grasp the back half of the wing and pull it rearward.

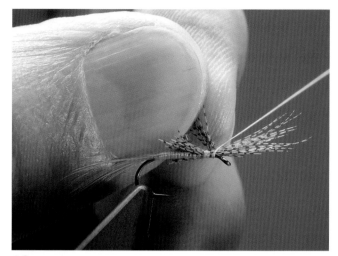

19. Bring thread once again through the gap.

20. The separated wings.

21. Alternately lifting one wing and then the other, make figure-eight wraps around their bases to secure them in their separated position.

Dry Flies

48

22. Wind thread rearward over the wing butts to form a smooth base for the body, and leave the thread hanging at the bend.

23. Apply dubbing to the hanging thread, thicker toward the bottom and sparser toward the top, so that when wound on the hook, the strand will form a tapered body.

24. Wind the dubbing forward, stopping short of the eye so you have room to wind the hackle.

25. Select a light ginger hackle feather about this size.

26. Tie in the hackle by its stem just behind the wing, leaving a bit of the stem protruding to get a secure tie-in.

49

27. Bind down the stem tip with wraps forward of the wing.

28. Wind the hackle three times behind the wing . . .

29. . . . and twice in front of the wing.

30. Whip finish.

31. The completed Light Cahill illustrates the classic Catskill dry fly architecture. Note the proportion of tail, body, and hackle to hook length and gap, and aim for such a profile whenever you tie this pattern style.

Hook	Standard dry fly, size 12–18
Thread	Light olive 6/0 (70 denier)
Tail	Medium blue dun spade hackle fibers
Wings	A pair of medium blue hen hackle tips
Body	One or two olive-dyed quills (depending on hook size)
Hackle	Medium blue dun

This pattern was developed by A. K. Best, the innovative professional from Colorado, author of *Production Fly Tying* (Pruett Publishing, 2003) and several other valuable books. Best is known for his exacting variations of mayfly dressings, and his quill-bodied flies have been widely imitated. To clarify, "quill" is also used to refer to sections of feather, as in quill-winged patterns, but in this case, quill means the stem of a hackle feather. This stem is wrapped around the hook, producing a body that is different from a dubbed body in two significant ways: it has a segmented look and it is slimmer than a dubbed body, both of which make it more realistic.

You can prepare a quill by stripping the barbs off a long hackle feather from the back of a cape, but you will then need to dye it, as the stripping process pulls off the outer layer of the quill, exposing its white core. It's simpler to buy dyed quills in the colors you need.

Soaking them in water will soften them up for easier winding around the hook.

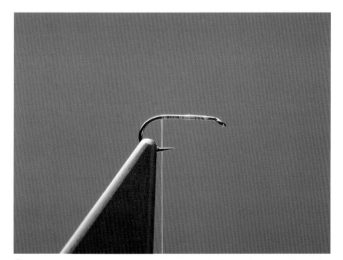

1. Tie on behind the eye and wind thread to the bend.

2. Select a spade hackle feather for tail material.

Dry Flies

3. Strip a small bundle of barbs from the hackle feather and tie it in at the bend, leaving a tail about one hook-shank long.

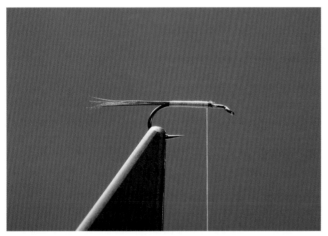

4. Wind the thread forward over the butts to a point one-third of the hook shank from the eye, and trim the waste.

5. Prepare two hen hackle tips for wings by stroking the unused barbs rearward until the tip sections are one hook-shank long.

6. Holding the hackle tips side-by-side so the ends flare out from each other, tie them in at the one-third point (where the thread is hanging) with a pinch wrap.

7. Wind the thread rearward three or four wraps over the stems to bind them down, and trim the waste.

8. Wind the thread forward to the wing, lift the wing, and make a few winds in front of it to prop it upright in the position shown.

9. View from the front, showing the spread of the wings.

10. Strip the barbs from the stem (quill) of an olive-dyed hackle feather, tie it in by the tip at the bend, then wind thread forward over the quill to the wing to bind it down.

Material Tip

Remember that quills are brittle and that soaking them in water will make them easier to wind without breaking. Do not—as sometimes recommended—add hair conditioner to the water. Although this will help soften the quills, it will also cause water to wick into the stem when you fish the fly, causing it to sink.

11. Grasping the tip of the quill with your thumb and forefinger (not hackle pliers), wind it forward in closely spaced wraps, stopping short enough of the wing to leave room for the hackle. Tie off and trim waste.

12. Tie in the hackle feather just behind the wing, and advance the thread to the eye.

13. Wind the hackle behind and then in front of the wing, and tie off the hackle.

14. Tie off the hackle, trim the waste, and whip finish. Comparing the completed Olive Dun Quill to a dubbed mayfly pattern like the Light Cahill (page 50) illustrates the two distinctive features of a quill body: slimness and segmentation. Because they are truer imitations of most mayfly bodies, quill-bodied flies can be the key to success when trout are feeding selectively.

Hook	Standard dry fly, size 18–24
Thread	Black 6/0 (70 denier) or 8/0
Tail	White Microfibbets
Wing	White turkey flat
Body	Black dubbing
Hackle	Black

"Trico" is short for *Tricorythodes*, a genus of very small mayflies that hatch profusely in late summer to early fall in both East and West. Given their wide distribution, great numbers, and long hatching span, you'd think everyone would be tying Tricos. In fact, this hatch may infuriate more anglers than it delights because these tiny flies, both real and imitation, are almost impossible to see on the water. One exception is during a spinner fall, when clouds of Tricos can be seen in the air and on the surface. For more on tying Tricos and variations, see Ed Engle's superb *Tying Small Flies* (Stackpole Books, 2004).

The pattern shown here is for a male dun. Note that it calls for a tail made from Microfibbets, which are just synthetic paint-brush bristles dyed various colors. They make excellent tailing material, especially for small mayfly imitations. The wing is made from a turkey feather called a "flat," so named because the top of the feather is flat.

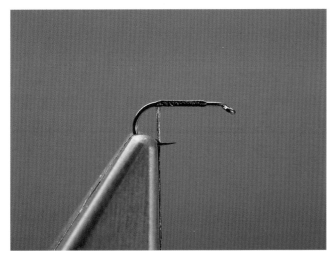

1. Before tying on, cut off an 8-inch length of thread and set it aside for step 3. Then, start thread behind the eye and wind to the bend.

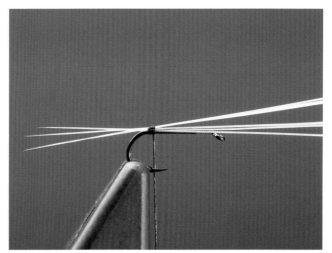

2. Tie in five or six Microfibbets at the bend so that the tail is one shank-length long.

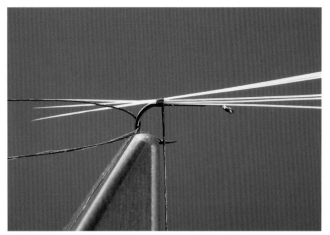

3. Loop the 8-inch piece of scrap thread around the bend in the hook.

4. With your fingernail, press down on the top of the Microfibbets so they spread apart, and position the scrap of thread in the middle, so as to create a forked tail.

5. Take two turns of working thread over the loop to hold it in place and then pull the loop toward the eye to spread the tails.

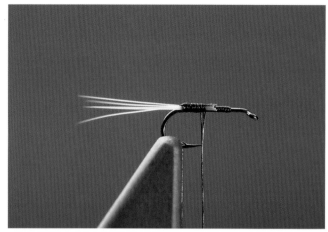

6. Make four or five wraps of working thread over the tail butts and scrap thread to secure them, and then trim the waste.

7. For the wing, cut a section of turkey flat that is four times the width of the hook gap.

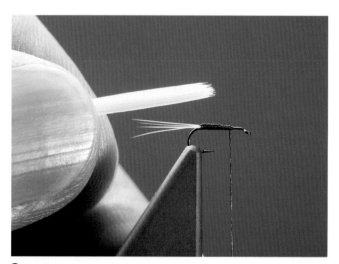

8. After cutting the section from the flat, square the tips by stroking it lengthwise. Then fold the section in half once and once again, resulting in a piece that is one hook-gap wide.

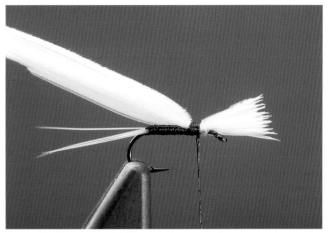

9. Tie in the wing at the one-third point, with feather tips pointing over the eye. The wing should be one hook-shank long.

10. Wind thread rearward over the wing butts and trim them parallel to the hook shank, so the body will be tapered when dubbed.

11. Lift the wing and take a few wraps in front of it to hold it upright. Trim the wing butts.

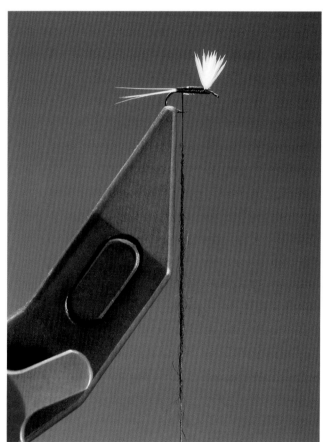

12. Wind back to the bend, pull the bobbin down and apply a sparse amount of dubbing to the thread.

13. Wrap the dubbing forward, stopping where shown to leave room for a hackle collar.

15. Wind the hackle two turns behind the wing and as many turns in front as it takes to fill the space.

14. Tie in a black hackle, by its stem, behind the wing.

16. Trim the waste hackle and whip finish. The finished Trico. Tie these in the smallest sizes you can manage, and watch for Trico hatches in late summer and early fall, when little else is happening.

Dry Flies

Attractor or "searching" dry fly patterns are those that imitate no specific insect but apparently look edible enough to the trout. It's impossible to know if a particular pattern imitates something the trout have seen recently or if the pattern just looks good to eat, but certain attractor patterns continue to catch fish in a wide a variety of places and times, which is argument enough for carrying them. Attractor patterns are particularly useful in two situations: when you want to search a promising stretch of water where no insects are evident, or when fish are rising to an insect you can't match with anything in your box.

Royal Wulff   Difficulty: Moderate

Hook	Standard dry fly, size 10–16
Thread	White and black 6/0 (70 denier)
Wings	White calf tail
Tail	Black moose body hair
Butt	Peacock herl
Body	Red floss
Shoulder	Peacock herl
Hackle	Brown

You've got to love that Lee Wulff called this creation "strawberry shortcake," meaning that to the fish, it looks just like an irresistible dessert. But it keeps on catching fish in all its variations, including the White Wulff, with white body, hackle, and tail, and the Ausable Wulff, with orange body and brown/grizzly hackle, developed by Fran Betters to fish the Ausable River in upstate New York. There are several more patterns based on the original, and you can experiment with your own.

The signature feature on all variations is the divided hair wings, whether of calf, elk, moose, or bucktail, but this is also the trickiest part of the fly to construct. Calf tail, the material used in the Royal Wulff, is crinkly and hard to stack, so your first few wings may be rather messy. Fear not: The bugginess of this fly is part of its appeal to the trout.

Note: Two colors of thread are used in this pattern: white in steps 1–6 to blend with the wing, and black for the rest of the fly.

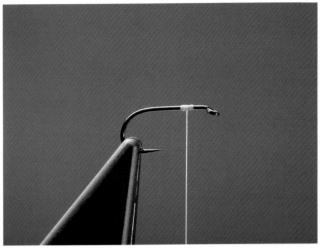

1. Start the thread ⅓ shank-length behind the eye.

2. Prepare a bundle of calf tail for the wing.

Material Tip

Calf tail is more crinkly than calf body hair, but it makes a better wing. To get the same look using body hair, you need a lot more material.

3. Tie in wing at the one-third point using a pinch wrap.

4. Wrap thread rearward three or four turns, and trim the waste calf tail at an angle sloping rearward, so body will be tapered when you wind thread over the stubs.

5. Wrap thread rearward over the wing stubs, then forward to where you tied in the wing. Note the tapered shape of the body.

6. Use cross winds to separate and define the wings, and then make two winds around each bundle to tighten it.

7. Whip finish the white thread in front of the wing and trim waste. Tie on the black thread near the mid-point of the shank, where the white thread ends, and wrap forward to the bend.

8. For the tail, stack a bundle of moose hair one hook-shank long and tie it in at the bend.

Material Tip

Moose hair is ideal tailing material: It's stiff, durable, and doesn't flare.

9. Trim the tail butts at an angle, then wrap thread forward over them to where the white thread ends, forming a smooth body.

10. Return thread to the bend, and tie in a peacock herl at the bend.

Material Tip

Herls vary in width. Wider ones are found near the base of a peacock tail feather and narrower ones toward the tip. Choose a herl that fits the size fly you're tying. (See page 8.)

11. Wrap the herl forward to form a collar about ⅓ the body length, and trim the waste.

12. Wrap the thread forward about ⅓ the body length (midway between herl and wing), and tie in a strand of red floss.

13. Wind red floss rearward, to the herl, and then back to the tie-in point, to form the red body.

14. After trimming the floss, tie in a second peacock herl where the black thread is hanging in the previous step. Wind the herl forward to form a collar the same size as the rear one, leaving enough space in front of it to tie in hackle.

15. Tie in a brown hackle feather, by its stem, behind the wing . . .

16. . . . and bind the stem in front of the wing to hold it down.

17. Wind three turns of hackle behind the wing and the remaining turns in front of the wing. Trim hackle and whip finish.

18. The completed Royal Wulff. Something about this pattern, whether it's the buggy wings or the flashy, segmented body, continues to attract trout in a wide variety of situations and locales.

Hook	Standard dry fly, size 10–16
Thread	Chartreuse (or red or orange) 6/0 nylon (70 denier)
Tail	Moose body hair
Wings	Deer body hair
Body	Working thread wound over butts of wings
Hackle	Brown

Guides and veterans swear by Humpies as searching dry fly patterns, yet many tiers never attempt them because of their reputation for being difficult. Once you get the feel for managing the deer-hair body—the hump—nothing else about this pattern should be problematic. It's effective in a range of sizes and colors, and depending on those variables, trout may take it for a mayfly, a caddisfly, or a terrestrial, from ant to beetle to grasshopper.

Two problems tiers mention most often about making the deer-hair hump are (1) estimating the right-size clump of hair to use, and (2) keeping the hair from migrating forward on the shank as they tie. Experience will solve the first problem, and we recommend tying several Humpies at one sitting so you retain what you learn from each misjudgment. Securely wrapping down the deer-hair bundle from the beginning will help solve the second problem.

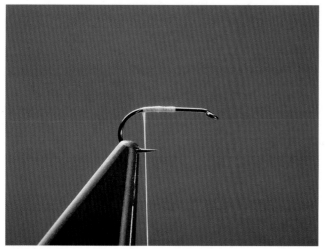

1. Start the thread at the midpoint of the shank and wind to the bend.

2. Tie in a stacked bundle of moose hair so the tail extends one shank-length to the rear.

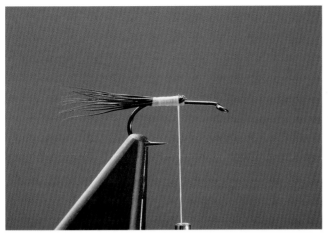

3. Wrap the thread forward to the starting point, binding down the moose hair butts, and trim the waste.

4. Build a thread base by wrapping back and forth between the midpoint and bend, and let the thread hang at the midpoint.

5. Cut and stack a bundle of deer hair for the wing. The right size bundle is critical when tying Humpies but difficult to estimate. Only experience will give you a feel for the right amount to use. Hold the bundle so its tips are aligned with the tips of the tail and you're gripping the bundle directly above the eye.

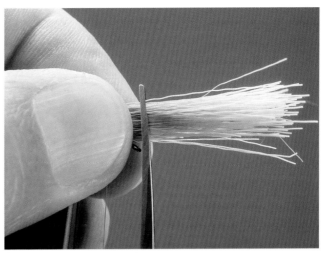

6. Cut the bundle where you're gripping it. You should now have a bundle that extends from the tips of the tail to the eye of the hook.

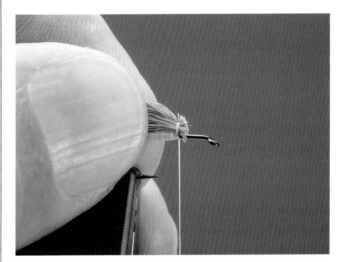

7. Tie in the bundle at the midpoint.

8. Wind the thread back to the bend in tight, close wraps to where the tail is tied in.

65

9. Fold the unbound portion of deer hair forward to the midpoint (where you started the thread in step 1).

10. Wind the thread forward to ⅓ shank-length behind the eye.

11. Grasp the near half of the deer-hair clump and take two turns of thread around it.

12. Grasp the far half and do the same around this clump.

13. Take two additional wraps around each wing to bind each one together.

14. Tie in two hackle feathers, one brown and one grizzly, by their stems and advance the thread to the eye.

15. Wrap grizzly hackle forward to just behind the eye, and secure it with two wraps of thread. Do not trim the hackle tip yet.

16. Wrap the brown hackle forward over the grizzly hackle, secure it with two wraps of thread, trim waste, and whip finish. Your first few Humpies may not look as neat and well proportioned as this one, but remember that estimating the right amount of deer hair to use is the key and is soon learned through trial and error.

Dry Flies

Parachute patterns introduced a major change in the architecture of the dry fly: Instead of the hackle being wound like a collar around the hook shank, a parachute hackle is wound around a single, vertical wingpost, sometimes called a parachute post. This orientation spreads the hackle fibers out in a circle in the same plane as the water (rather than perpendicular to it) and allows the fly's body to lie down on the water rather than up on its hackle tips. A traditional dry fly, by contrast, sits up on its hackle tips and tail, with the body just out of the water. The low-lying parachute is thought to more realistically imitate the way a mayfly dun sits on the water, and thus is more effective in flat pools where the trout get a good look at flies drifting by.

Although a parachute's low profile makes it somewhat harder for the angler to follow on the water than a high-riding Catskill dry, this problem is overcome by using a bright color, such as white, chartreuse, or even pink, for the wingpost. The trout don't seem to care.

Parachute Adams   Difficulty: Moderate

Hook	Standard dry fly, size 12–20
Thread	Black or gray 6/0 (70 denier)
Wingpost	White poly yarn (or calf body hair)*
Tail	Moose body hair
Body	Muskrat dubbing
Hackle	Grizzly

If you were restricted to carrying just one dry fly pattern, this might be the best choice of all. In color and shape, it resembles so many mayflies and caddisflies that it will almost always catch fish when duns of these insects are on the water, as long as you have the right size.

The Adams was created by Len Halladay of Michigan in 1922, and is still a standard in most fly boxes, but the parachute version may be even more effective, especially in pools and smooth runs. Tie them by the dozen in several sizes.

*The traditional recipe calls for calf body hair for the wingpost, but poly yarn is much easier to work with and is also less bulky, an advantage in tying the pattern in smaller sizes.

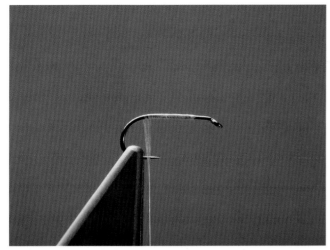

1. Tie in at one-third point and wrap thread rearward to bend.

2. Tie in a stacked bundle of moose hair at the bend to create a tail one shank-length long.

3. Wrap the thread forward to the tie-in point and trim the waste hair.

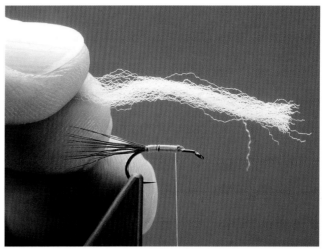

4. Cut a 3-inch piece of poly yarn for the wingpost. If you are tying the pattern in a small size, you may have to pick out some fibers to get a strand of appropriate diameter.

5. Tie in the piece of yarn at the one-third point, perpendicular to the hook shank, with diagonal cross winds. (See X-Wrap instructions, p. 118.)

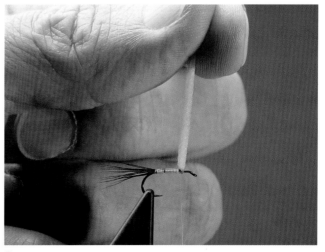

6. Lift both wings . . .

7. . . . and wrap thread around their bases. This forms the wingpost around which the parachute hackle will be wound.

8. Tie the grizzly hackle stem on the hook shank, in front of the wingpost.

9. Bind the hackle stem to the wingpost by wrapping thread around both the hackle stem and the wingpost.

Material Tip

A common mistake in making small dry flies is putting too much dubbing on the thread. You'll need less than you think.

10. Wind rearward to the midpoint, let the bobbin hang, and apply a sparse strand of dubbing to the thread.

11. Wind the dubbing forward to the eye.

12. Grasping the tip of the feather with hackle pliers, wind hackle around the wingpost.

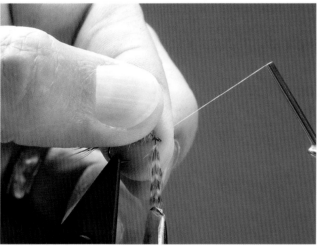

13. Pull the wing back and trap the hackle with a turn of thread.

14. Make a couple more turns of thread around the hackle, and trim the waste.

15. Whip finish.

16. Pull the wingpost upright and trim until it is one shank-length long.

17. Apply a drop of flexible cement where hackle meets wing to keep the wing in position and the hackle from unwinding.

18. The completed Parachute Adams. Compare the profile of this pattern to that of a traditional dry fly (such as the Light Cahill or Olive Dun Quill) and it's evident why the parachute style rides lower in the water: there's no hackle collar to prop it up. Still, a Parachute Adams treated with floatant will stay afloat through many drifts, and the bright white wingpost will keep the fly visible to the angler.

Although mayflies long got the bulk of the attention from fly fishers and fly tiers, trout everywhere feed on caddisflies in all their forms—larva, pupa, and adult. The late Gary LaFontaine studied these insects extensively, and his *Caddisflies* (Lyons Press, 1981) is still the definitive work on the subject.

The most obvious difference between a mayfly dun and caddisfly adult is that the wings of the mayfly stand upright at rest, whereas those of the caddisfly fold over its body like a moth's. Another difference is that caddisflies occur in a more limited range of colors—all drab shades of brown and grayish brown—than mayflies.

Creators of caddis dry fly patterns have found various ways of suggesting the folded-wing shape, the simplest solution being to use hair for the wings, as in Al Troth's classic Elk Hair Caddis. The two patterns shown here represent alternative ways of creating the caddisfly shape, one using feather wings (Henryville Special), and the other, a body of spun and clipped deer hair (Goddard Caddis).

When fishing caddisfly drys on faster water, keep in mind that some types of caddis adults skitter and hop after emerging. Whenever you see and hear trout slashing the surface in noisy takes, it's a good bet they're feeding on jumpy caddis, and in such situations, twitching your fly will often trigger strikes. The two patterns shown here are high-riding flies that work well with this technique.

Henryville Special   Difficulty: Moderate

Hook	Standard dry fly, size 12–20
Thread	Black 6/0 nylon (70 denier)
Rib	Fine gold wire
Body	Olive fur or synthetic dubbing
Hackle	Grizzly
Underwing	Lemon barred wood duck flank fibers
Wing	Mallard feather section
Hackle	Dark ginger or light brown

The originator of this pattern is unknown. According to Gary LaFontaine, Pennsylvania fisherman Hiram Brobst came across the pattern in an old British fly-fishing book and adapted it for fishing caddisfly hatches on the Brodhead River in the Poconos. It is named after a section of that river. The pattern is especially effective when active adults are hatching or when the females are flying low over the stream depositing their eggs.

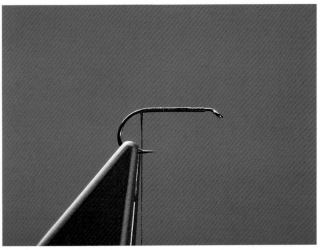

1. Tie on an eye's width behind the eye (to leave room for the head) and wind forward to the bend.

4. Bend the wire stub back toward the bend of the hook.

2. Tie in a 3- or 4-inch length of gold wire at the bend and advance it to the midpoint.

5. Wrap thread rearward over this stub to securely anchor it.

3. Trim the wire, leaving a short stub (so you can secure the wire to the hook in the next two steps).

6. Select a grizzly hackle feather one size smaller than you would for the same size dry fly, and tie it in by the stem at the bend.

7. Dub the thread.

8. Wind dubbing forward to a point ⅓ shank-length from the eye.

9. Wind the hackle forward to the front of the body in widely spaced spirals, a technique known as "palmered" hackle.

10. Counterwind the wire (i.e., wrap it in a different direction around the hook than you did the hackle) forward to the front of the body. If you trap any hackle barbs in the process, pick them out with your bodkin.

11. Tie in a bundle of wood duck barbs a full hook-length long (not a shank-length) for the underwing. Trim off the waste (forward section).

14. Fold the section in half, lengthwise, and tie it in behind the eye with the notched end pointing rearward.

12. Cut a section of mallard feather and coat it with flexible cement to prevent splitting.

15. After trimming the butt ends of the mallard section, tie in a ginger (or light brown) hackle feather by its stem at the same point you tied in the mallard.

13. Square off one end of the section and cut a V–shaped notch in it.

16. Wind the ginger hackle forward in tight wraps toward the eye.

17. Whip finish, and trim the waste. The Henryville Special is a good, general caddisfly pattern in any situation. According to Gray LaFontaine, its key feature is that it "suggests motion even when it is drifting dead with the current." And remember that twitching this fly will often trigger strikes from trout keying in on hatching caddisflies.

Hook	Standard dry fly, size 10–18
Thread	Black 6/0 and 3/0 (70 and 140 denier)
Body	Spun and clipped deer or caribou hair
Antennae	Brown hackle stems
Hackle	Brown

This pattern is the invention of British fly fisherman and author John Goddard, who, with Brian Clarke, wrote the definitive work on how trout see, *The Trout and the Fly* (Ernest Benn, 1980). The distinguishing feature of the pattern is the spun and clipped deer-hair body, sculpted to imitate the caddisfly profile. This feature, along with the ample hackle collar, makes it float like a cork, and so it's a great dressing for rough water. According to Dave Hughes, it also works well on flat water.

Note that two weights of thread are prescribed for this pattern, the heavier for binding down the bundles of deer hair.

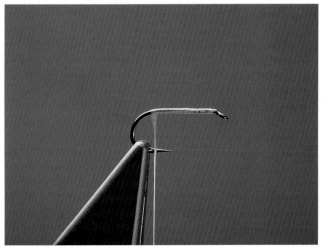

1. Tie on 3/0 (140 denier) thread at the eye and wind rearward to bend.

2. Cut a bundle of deer hair from the hide.

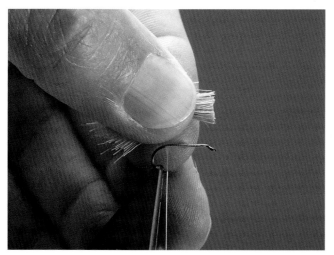

3. Trim the tips even.

4. Tie in the bundle at the bend. First make two loose wraps, snug them up, and then as you begin to tighten the thread with your bobbin hand, release the bundle with your other hand. After the hair flares, make two more tight wraps of thread in the same place.

5. Form a triangle with the thumb and forefinger of your left hand.

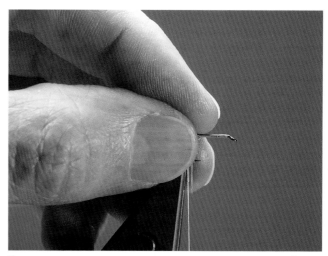

6. Slide this triangle of fingers rearward over the bundle of deer hair, pulling it back, and make two wraps of thread in front of the bundle.

7. Prepare a second bundle of deer hair. Hold it at a 45-degree angle over the shank in front of the first bunch.

8. Tie it down so it flares, as with the first bundle.

9. Compress the two bundles by pushing in from both sides with thumb and forefinger of each hand.

10. Prepare and tie on a third bundle (and a fourth, if necessary) until you have covered two-thirds of the shank with flared deer hair. Whip finish and trim thread waste.

11. Remove the fly from the vise and begin trimming the body . . .

12. . . . by cutting the hairs on the bottom . . .

13. . . . until the bottom is flat.

14. Continue trimming until the body has this shape.

15. Trim the rear of the body into the shape of a cad-disfly with folded wings.

16. Tie on 70 denier thread in front of the deer-hair body. To make antennae, strip the barbs off two rooster hackles from the butt end of a cape (hackles you'd never use for anything else).

17. Tie in the stripped hackles in front of the deer hair, on top of the hook, and trim the ends so the antennae are twice the shank length.

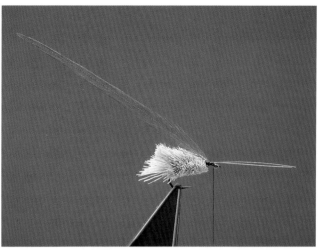

18. Tie in a brown hackle, by its stem, behind the eye.

19. Wind the hackle forward in tight turns, each one abutting its neighbor.

20. Tie down the hackle, trim the waste, and whip finish to complete the Goddard Caddis.

Stoneflies are the third main order of aquatic insect, after mayflies and caddisflies, on which trout feed. They have long, flat wings held against their bodies when at rest, and so are immediately distinguishable from the other two types. They also behave differently, spending less time in the air. Rather than floating to the surface, stonefly nymphs crawl out of the water onto the bank to shed their cases, which can often be found on streamside rocks. The adults spend most of their time in streamside vegetation, though the females return to the water to deposit their eggs, at which time they are most vulnerable to trout.

Stimulator   Difficulty: Moderate

Hook	3X or 4X long, size 6–10
Thread	Orange 6/0 nylon (70 denier)
Tail	Elk body hair
Rib	Grizzly hackle
Abdomen	Rust dubbing or Kaufmann's Stimulator dubbing, golden
Wing	Elk body hair
Thorax	Orange dubbing or Kaufmann's Stimulator dubbing, flame
Hackle	Grizzly

This Randall Kaufmann creation, originally designed for the giant salmon fly and golden stonefly hatches on western rivers, has proven to be a great attractor pattern that works wherever down-wing insects, including stoneflies, caddisflies, and grasshoppers, are present. It is therefore tied in a wide range of sizes and colors.

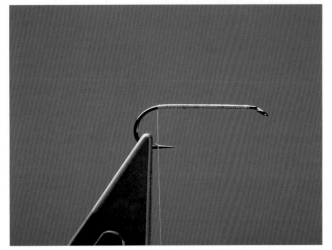

1. Tie on behind the eye and wind to the bend.

2. Cut and stack a small bundle of elk hair and tie it in at the bend for a tail. The tail should be ½ shank-length.

3. Bind down the butts of the elk hair, wrapping back and forth over them for two-thirds of the shank. Trim the waste.

4. Wrap the thread back to the bend and tie in a grizzly hackle there.

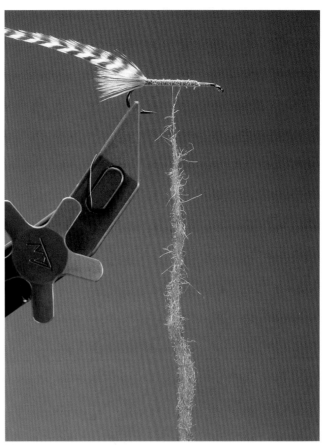

5. Move the thread to the midpoint and apply dubbing to make the abdomen.

6. Wind the dubbing forward to create an abdomen ⅔ shank-length.

7. Wind the hackle forward, palmer-style, to the forward point of the abdomen. Tie it off and trim the waste.

8. Cut and stack a second bundle of elk hair, slightly larger than the tail bundle, to use as a wing, and tie it in at the front of the body.

9. Wind forward over the butts to the eye, and trim the waste.

10. Tie in a second grizzly hackle, by its stem, in front of the wing.

11. Extend the thread and apply orange (or Kaufmann's Flame) dubbing to create a thorax.

12. Wrap the dubbing forward to the eye.

Technique Tip

To avoid cutting the working thread when trimming material in tight quarters (here, tidying up stray hackle), hold the thread out of the way with the little finger of your non-scissors hand.

13. Palmer the hackle forward over the thorax. Trim waste and whip finish to complete the Stimulator. The deer hair and palmered hackle make this pattern float like a cork, and it is therefore a good choice for rough water and for use with dropper flies.

Dry Flies

The spinner is the final stage of the mayfly's life, the slender-bodied, transparent-winged phase into which the duns transform before mating. The mating occurs in the air above the water, the act itself preceded by the males' up-and-down mating flight, which is the spinner activity anglers are most likely to observe. The females join the dancing males in the air, and after mating, fall to the surface of the water to deposit their eggs. They then lay spent on the surface of the water, where they are carried downstream and eaten by trout.

Although spinner falls can be dramatic—fish rising everywhere to masses of spent mayflies floating on the water—they can also be maddeningly hard to fish because the insects are so hard to see in this form, with their slender bodies and transparent wings flush to the surface. Compounding the problem is the fact that most spinner falls occur at dusk. Still, if you are on the water during a large spinner fall, you will die for a spinner pattern.

Rusty CDC Biot Spinner   Difficulty: Moderate

Hook	Standard dry fly, size 14–20
Thread	Brown 6/0 (70 denier) or 8/0 for very small sizes
Tails	Light blue dun Microfibbets or hackle fibers
Abdomen	Rusty brown turkey biot
Underwing	Light blue dun CDC feather with stem
Overwing	Light blue dun Z-lon
Thorax	Rusty fur or synthetic dubbing

John Gierach, as keen a student of aquatic insects as you'll find, says in *Good Flies* (Lyons Press, 2000) that "at least half" of the mayfly duns he observes transform into rusty-colored spinners. That in itself recommends this pattern. It's also worth noting that Gierach, a natural-materials advocate, concedes that imitating diaphanous spinner wings is one application where synthetics make sense. We therefore include this pattern as a good generic spinner imitation to carry—again, in several sizes, for that is usually the key—for those times when you find yourself on the water in the evening with trout everywhere sipping something you can't see. Look for the spinners on the surface and enter the fray.

Dry Flies

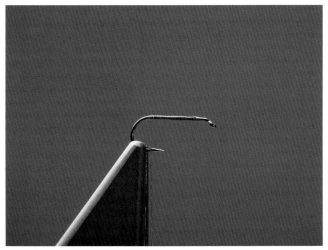

1. Cut an 8-inch scrap of thread and set it aside. Then tie in at the eye and wind to the bend.

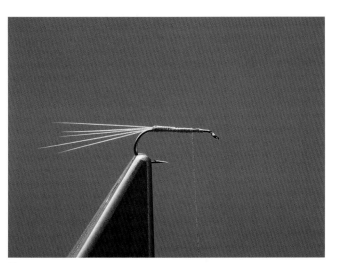

2. Tie in five Microfibbets at the bend and separate them using the technique shown on page 56. Wind thread forward to the one-third position.

3. Select two CDC feathers with stems.

4. To form the underwing, tie the CDC feathers in at the one-third point, one tip pointing left and one right.

5. Bind down the CDC stems and trim the waste.

Material Tip

CDC nipple plumes (oiler puffs), as used for the CDC Emerger, have no stems. In patterns like the Rusty CDC Biot Spinner, you need a CDC feather with a stem for the wings to hold their shape.

Dry Flies

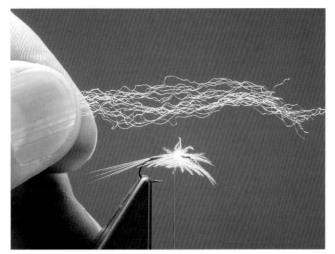

6. Strip some fibers from a length of Z-lon to make a sparse bundle.

7. Tie the length of Z-lon in on top of the underwing with an X-Wrap (p. 118).

8. Trim the Z-lon to the same length as the underwing.

9. Wind the thread back to the bend and tie in a rusty brown biot, with notch up. Advance the thread to the one-third point.

10. To form the body, wrap the biot forward to where the thread is hanging and tie it off there.

11. Trim the waste biot.

12. Apply a sparse amount of fine rusty brown dubbing.

13. Wind dubbing behind the wings and then around them in a figure-eight, ending with a wrap in front of the wings. Trim the waste and whip finish.

14. The finished Rusty CDC Biot Spinner. A key feature of any spinner pattern is the orientation of the wings perpendicular to the body. The wings in this pattern are special because of the combination of materials: The stemmed CDC feather gives the wings shape and provides flotation, while the Z-lon lends the diaphanous look of the real thing.

5

Terrestrials

Terrestrials are sometimes your best bet to catch trout. In late summer especially, when no insects are hatching, an ant or beetle cast near the bank may fetch trout all day, and a grasshopper may get you the biggest trout of the season. Trout eat terrestrials that have been blown or fallen into the river, rather than those that have emerged from its bottom; so, unlike aquatic insects, which are constantly available in one form or another and are part of the trout's regular feeding cycle, terrestrials are random opportunities. They sometimes catch fish when all else fails.

Vince Marinaro's *A Modern Dry Fly Code* (Lyons Press, 1997) was the first work to study terrestrial fishing for trout in detail, and includes recipes for several early patterns. His laboratory was the limestone streams of southeastern Pennsylvania, but what he observed has been applied to spring creeks everywhere. A second indispensable work is *Terrestrials* by Harrison Steeves and Ed Koch (Stackpole Books, 1994).

As fly patterns, terrestrials range from the easiest in the world to tie (simple ants and beetles) to among the most complex (grasshoppers, with their many body parts and tricky legs). You are missing some great action if you don't keep a few of each in your fly box.

Black Thread Ant

Dave's Hopper

Black Foam Beetle

Black Thread Ant

Difficulty: Easy

Hook	Standard dry fly, size 14–20
Thread	Black 6/0 (70 denier)
Abdomen and thorax	Working thread
Hackle	Black, soft and webby

This is a very simple pattern based on the sinking ant described in *Terrestrials* and credited to Bob McCafferty. If you prefer a floating ant, several simple patterns with foam or fur bodies are widely available. However, be warned that even floating ants can be difficult to see on the water because they are small and dark and ride down in the surface film. To increase their visibility, some patterns include bright indicator materials tied to the top of their bodies.

Because this pattern is intended to be fished wet, the hackle, which represents the ant's legs, should be soft and webby.

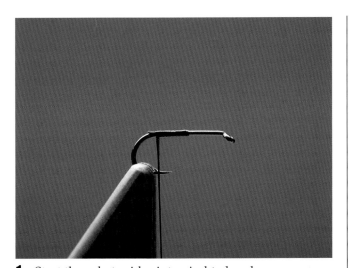

1. Start thread at midpoint, wind to bend.

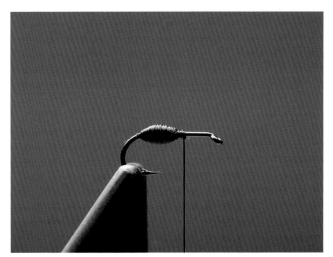

2. Continue winding back and forth to form an abdomen that's fat in the middle and tapered on the ends.

Technique Tip

If your thread begins to slide off the wrap beneath it as you wind, spin the bobbin counterclockwise to flatten the thread.

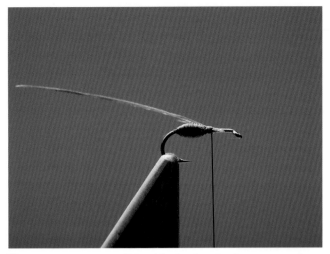

3. Tie in a very small hackle feather by its stem at the midpoint, just forward of the abdomen.

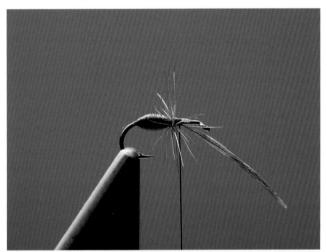

4. Wind the hackle three turns toward the eye. The barbs here imitate legs, and an ant only has six, so you don't want a thick collar.

5. Trim off the hackle tip.

6. Using the same technique as for the abdomen, wind back and forth between the hackle and eye to form a thorax. This lump should be slightly smaller than the abdomen.

7. Whip finish and coat the entire body with head cement to complete the Black Thread Ant.

Black Foam Beetle

Hook	Standard dry fly, size 12–18
Thread	Black 6/0 (70 denier)
Carapace	Black closed-cell foam
Body	Peacock herl
Legs	Round rubber, black
Indicator	Bright orange or chartreuse poly yarn

This beetle is very simple to tie but very effective. The key ingredient, according to Dave Hughes, is the body of closed-cell foam (switch-plate insulators are a cheap and handy source), which allows the fly to drift in the surface film, where it belongs, without sinking.

The addition of the bright indicator will help you track the beetle's drift. The leg material is sold as "round rubber" in fly-tying catalogs and shops.

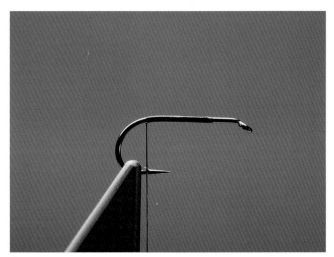

1. Start thread at the one-third position and wind to the bend.

2. A switch-plate insulator is a good source of foam for this pattern.

93

3. Cut a strip of foam one hook-gap wide and trim one end to a point.

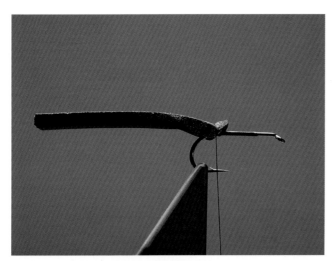

4. Tie the pointed end in at the bend.

5. At the same place, tie in five or six peacock herls by their tips.

6. Twist the herls counterclockwise into a strand.

7. Wind the twisted herl strand forward to the tie-in point and trim waste.

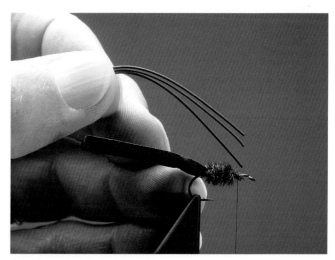

8. Select three strands of round rubber.

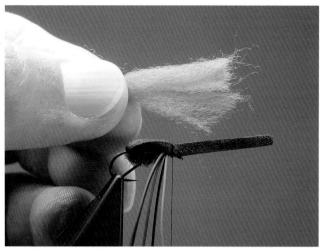

11. Take a piece of poly yarn and pull the fibers apart.

9. Tie in the three strands at their midpoints, just behind the eye, with cross-winds so they're perpendicular to the hook shank.

12. Tie the yarn in at its midpoint on top of the foam, behind the legs.

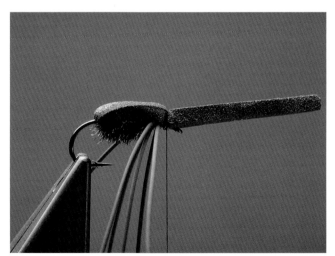

10. Advance thread in front of the legs, fold the foam strip forward over the body, and tie it down with three wraps of thread.

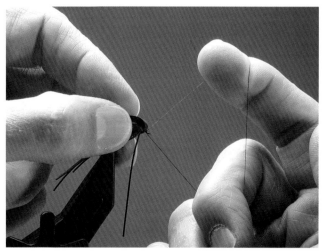

13. Lift the foam and throw a whip finish at the eye of the hook.

14. Trim the top of the yarn.

15. Trim the foam even with the eye of the hook.

16. Pull the legs up . . .

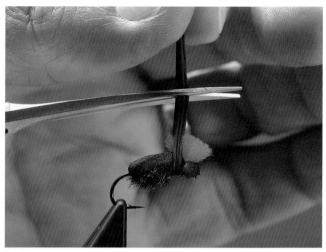

17. . . . and trim them so they're one hook-shank long.

18. The completed Black Foam Beetle.

19. Overhead view, showing legs.

Dave's Hopper

Difficulty: Hard

Hook	2X or 3X long, size 6–14
Thread	Brown 70 denier
Tail	Red-dyed deer hair
Ribbing hackle	
	Brown
Body	Yellow yarn
Underwing	Pale yellow–dyed deer hair
Wing	Mottled turkey wing or tail feather section
Legs	Yellow-dyed grizzly hackle stems, knotted
Collar	Tips of deer-hair head fibers
Head	Deer hair

Historical note: This pattern was created by Dave Whitlock, although the addition of legs was the suggestion of veteran tier Jay Buchner of Jackson, Wyoming, and this version is sometimes referred to as Jay-Dave's Hopper.

Fishing a pattern of this bulk demands an adjustment for dry fly fishermen. Vince Marinaro discovered two key points about fishing hoppers. First, whereas with a dry fly you want a slack leader to get a drag-free drift, Marinaro accidentally discovered that fishing a hopper on a taut leader though rippling water was the best way to get it to twitch and bob like the real thing—more lifelike movement than twitching it with rod or line. Second, he found that casting to individual fish and letting the hopper splat down on the water near them often triggered strikes, as trout often lie in wait for grasshoppers to land.

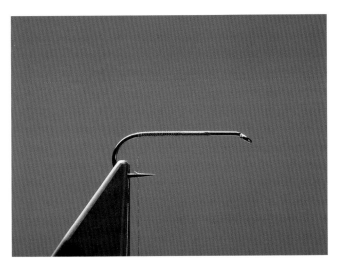

1. Tie in at a point ¼ shank-length from the eye and wind back to the bend.

2. Stack a bundle of red deer hair and tie it in at the bend with a portion ⅓ shank long extending to the rear.

3. Prepare a long brown rooster hackle by stroking back the barbs perpendicular to the stem, then trimming the barbs on each side so they are ½ hook-gap in length.

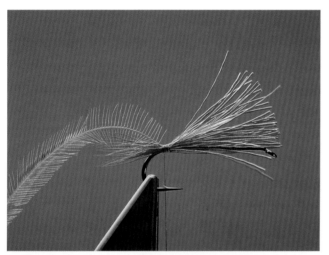

4. Tie in the hackle by the tip at the tail position.

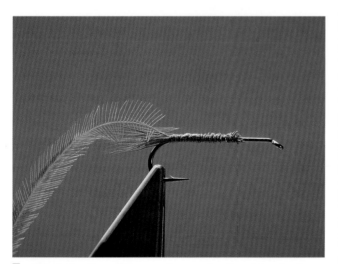

5. Wind the thread forward over the tip of the feather and the deer hair until you reach the tie-in point.

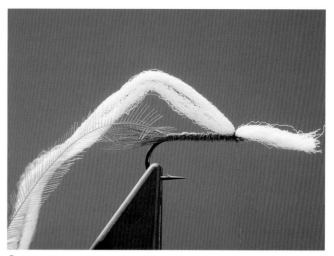

6. Tie in the piece of yellow yarn.

7. Wind the thread rearward to the tail, binding down the yarn.

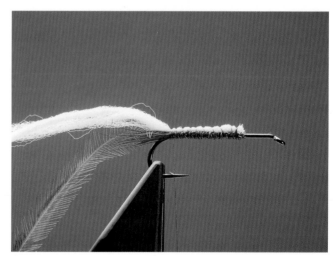

8. Trim the waste from the forward end of the yarn.

9. Fold the yarn forward, leaving a small loop at the rear, half the length of the tail. Bind down the loop with four or five tight wraps of thread.

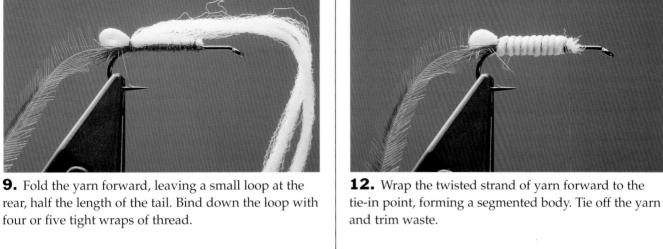

12. Wrap the twisted strand of yarn forward to the tie-in point, forming a segmented body. Tie off the yarn and trim waste.

10. Advance the thread to the tie-in point.

13. Wind hackle forward through the segments to the front of the body. Tie off and trim.

11. Twist the loose strand of yarn tightly counter-clockwise.

14. To make the underwing, cut and stack a small bunch of yellow deer hair. Hold it over the hook, as shown, to gauge the length: It should extend from the front of the body to the end of the tail.

15. Tie in the bundle of yellow deer hair in front of the body and trim the waste.

16. Select a section of turkey tail feather one hook-gap wide, coat it with flexible cement, and trim the tip of the feather square . . .

17. . . . and then round the corners on the tip.

18. Tie in the turkey feather over the underwing with the trimmed tip pointing rearward, and trim the waste.

19. To make one leg, select a yellow-dyed grizzly hackle feather.

20. Stroke the barbs back perpendicular to the stem.

21. Trim the barbs on each side down to stubble.

22. Tie an overhand knot in the top of the feather, leaving a tag end of an inch or two.

23. Trim the tip to a length approximating this segment of a grasshopper's leg (tibia).

24. Position the leg as shown and tie it in at the front of the body.

25. Prepare and tie in the second leg. Trim the waste from the front of both legs.

26. To begin the head, cut a bundle of deer hair as long as the body, and stack it.

27. Align the tips with the end of the body, tie in the bundle behind the eye, and let it flare.

28. Add another bundle or two of deer hair until the space is filled, whip finish, and trim the waste thread.

29. Trim the bottom of the deer hair flat, taking care not to cut the collar—the rearward portion of the first bundle.

30. Cut the sides and top of the deer hair into a cube, again taking care not to cut the collar.

31. Round the top corners of the cube to give the head its final shape. The completed Dave's Hopper. No one procedure in this pattern is especially difficult, but it has more parts and more steps than most and so takes more time to build.

6

Streamers

Streamers perennially catch some of the biggest trout in the stream, even though most fly fishers use them far less than they do insect imitations. And therein lies the key: Big trout develop a taste for baitfish, and that's what streamers imitate. Some streamers, such as the Woolly Bugger, may also be taken for leeches or crayfish, but when you're fishing a streamer, you're usually trying to imitate a baitfish.

In *Spring Creeks*, veteran Montana guide Mike Lawson gives a valuable tip on streamer fishing by dividing baitfish into two categories: free-swimming and bottom-dwelling. The free-swimmers, such as dace, chubs, and baby trout, are generally too fast and wary for trout to catch. The trout know this and don't waste energy chas-

ing healthy specimens, focusing instead on individuals behaving erratically. Thus, when you see trout chasing free-swimming baitfish, or when you want to search a stretch of water for lunker trout, a dead drift followed by a twitching retrieve will often trigger strikes. The Zonker pattern below is a great choice for this kind of fishing.

The bottom-dwelling species most available to trout is the sculpin, which is not as fast or agile as a free-swimmer; it hugs the bottom and relies on camouflage for protection. Thus, when you fish a sculpin imitation, like the famous Muddler Minnow, bump it along the bottom like the real thing.

Zonker

Muddler Minnow

Hook	4X to 6X long, size 2–10
Thread	Red and black 6/0 (70 denier)
Wing	Rabbit fur strip or precut Zonker strip
Tail and body	
	Pearl or silver Mylar
Hackle	Grizzly

The Zonker was created by tier Dan Byford in the 1970s as a free-swimming baitfish imitation for big trout. It is was an immediate success and went on to become one of those patterns that tiers everywhere find infinitely variable. You now see Zonkers in many colors, with variations of flashy material and trim and in a wide range of sizes, including giant flies for pike, musky, and saltwater species. The popularity of the pattern has prompted fly shops and catalogs to stock prepared Zonker strips, precut lengths of dyed rabbit fur with the skin attached, in a number of sizes and colors.

In streams and rivers, Zonkers can be fished anywhere larger trout are likely to hang, including deeper pools and runs, pocket water, and undercut banks. Zonkers are also very effective in lakes, especially when used with sinking-tip or sinking lines to get them down to deeper water. In any situation, try an erratic retrieve to imitate an injured baitfish.

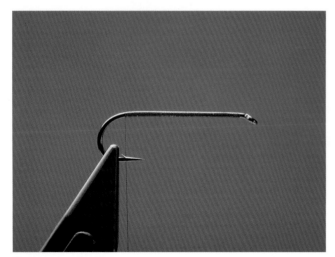

1. Tie on red thread at the eye and wind to the bend.

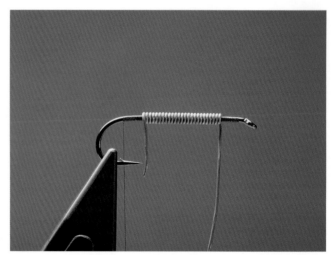

2. Wind weighting wire from above the point of the hook forward to the one-quarter point.

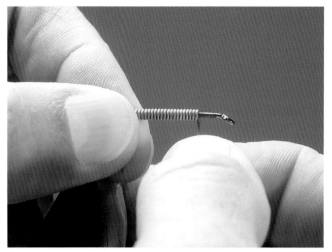

3. Trim the waste by pulling on the end of the wire until it breaks, rather than cutting it.

Technique Tip

Trimming thicker wire in this way leaves a tapered end that can be tucked neatly against the hook, resulting in no lumps when body material is wound over it.

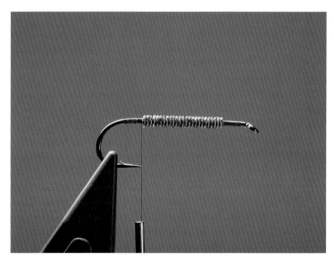

4. Wrap thread back and forth in wide spirals over the wire to bind it down.

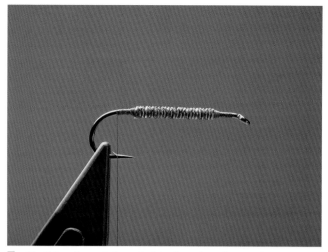

5. Build a thread dam behind and in front of the weighting wire to keep it from sliding forward or aft.

6. Tie in a piece of yarn forward of the weighting wire, underneath the hook shank.

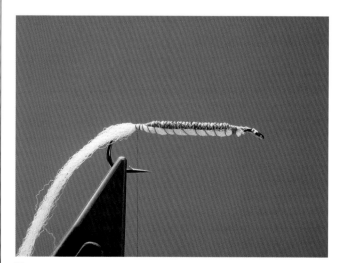

7. Bring yarn underneath shank and wind thread rearward to the bend. Trim the waste yarn in front.

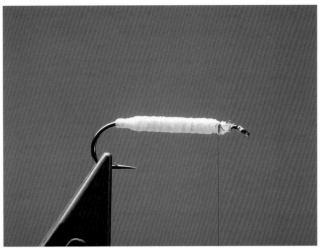

8. Wind the yarn forward over the wire and tie it off in front. Trim the waste, whip finish, and cut the waste end of thread.

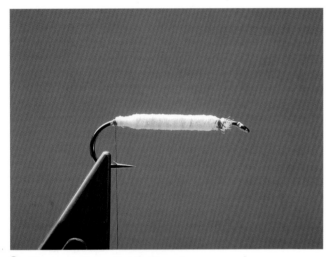

9. Reattach thread at the bend.

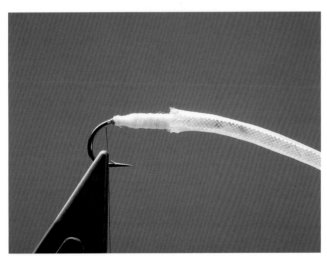

10. Slide a piece of Mylar tubing over the eye and push it rearward.

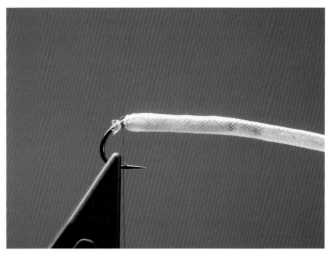

11. Secure the tubing at bend with several wraps of thread.

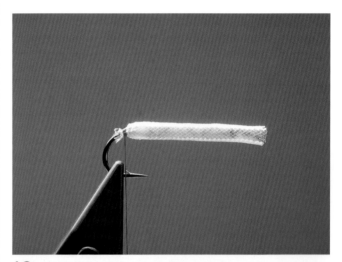

12. Cut off the front end of the tubing at the eye.

13. Select a grizzly Zonker strip.

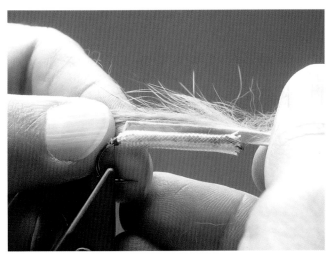

14. Hold the strip against the hook to measure a piece one hook-shank long.

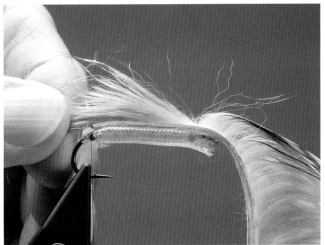

15. At the measured point, pull the fur forward to expose the skin. Moistening the fur with saliva will help keep it in place.

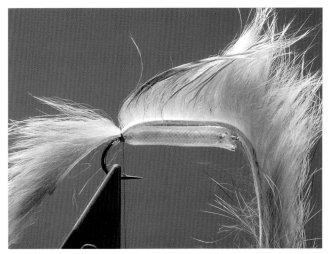

16. Position the strip with exposed skin over the bend, and tie it in.

17. Trim the forward end of the strip even with the eye of the hook.

18. Whip finish at the bend and apply head cement to the windings.

19. Pull the tubing rearward to expose the eye and tie on black thread.

20. Pull the tubing forward over the eye and bind it down in front of the weighting wire.

21. Trim off the waste tubing.

22. Bind down the Zonker strip in front of the weighting wire and trim the waste.

23. Prepare a grizzly hackle by stroking the barbs perpendicular to the stem.

24. Tie in the hackle in front of the body and pull a group of barbs toward the bend.

25. Trim the waste end of the tip.

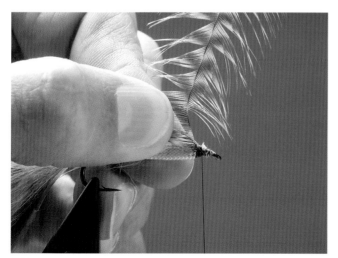

26. Lift the hackle and pull a group of barbs rearward.

27. Wind the hackle forward, and after each rotation, repeat the previous step—pulling barbs rearward—until you reach the eye.

28. Trim the hackle tip and whip finish. The Zonker is a flamboyant streamer that can attract big trout. Tie a few in large sizes—2 and 4—if you plan to go lunker hunting.

Streamers

Hook	Standard streamer, 3X or 4X long, size 2–12
Weight	Lead-free wire
Thread	Gray 3/0 (140 denier)
Tail	Mottled turkey feather
Body	Gold Mylar
Underwing	Gray squirrel tail
Wing	Mottled turkey feather sections
Collar	Deer hair
Head	Deer hair

This classic is at the top of most trout anglers' list of streamers. It was created by Minnesota tier Dan Gapen in the 1930s to imitate sculpin and fish for brook trout in Ontario's Nipigon River. Many beginning tiers find this a tricky pattern because of the paired wings and spun deer-hair head, but it is a must for the well-stocked fly box.

One of the inherent problems in fishing this fly as a sculpin imitation is that the deer-hair head makes the fly buoyant, even when wet. (Perhaps by accident, many anglers discover they can fish a floating Muddler as a grasshopper imitation.) But to fish it on the bottom as a sculpin, you need to add substantial weight, either with weighting wire and/or split shot. If you want a fly that will sink more quickly, with less weight, you might heed Mike Lawson's advice and tie the deer-hair head sparsely, as in Gapen's original.

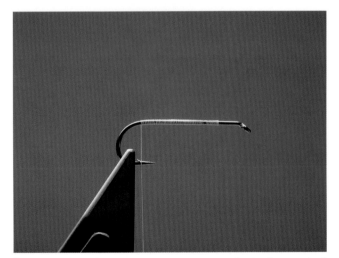

1. Start thread at one-quarter point and wind rearward to bend.

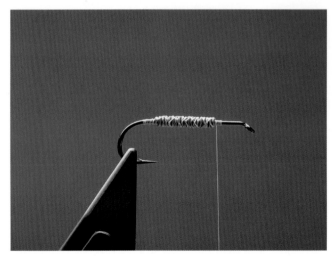

2. Wrap weighting wire from the hook point to ⅓ shank-length from the eye.

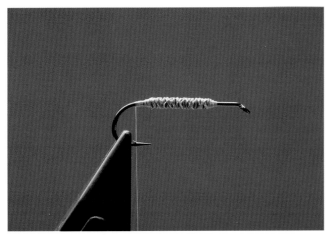

3. Build thread dams at each end of the weighting wire to keep it in place.

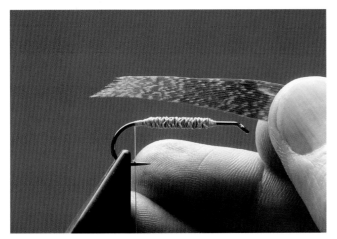

4. Cut a section of mottled turkey feather one hook-gap wide.

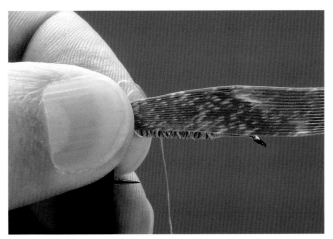

5. Make two loose loops of thread around the feather at the bend, holding the loops between thumb and forefinger and not letting them tighten.

6. Grasp the butt end (forward end) of the feather and release the two loose thread loops, still holding onto the feather, so the weight of the bobbin pulls the feather down onto the hook.

7. Trim the waste turkey feather and wrap the thread forward to the front of the body.

Cut a piece of Mylar (most tiers underestimate the length they'll need) and tie it in at the front of the body.

Material Tip

If your Mylar is gold on one side and silver on the other, tie it in with the gold side against the hook. When you wrap it, the gold side will be on the outside.

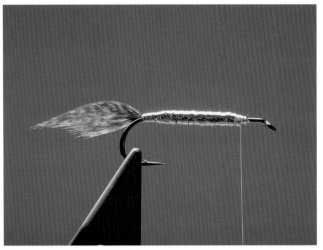

8. Wind the Mylar rearward in abutting wraps, gold side out, down to the tail and back, and trim the waste.

9. For the underwing, cut a bundle of hair from a squirrel tail, and comb out the underfur and short hairs. Set the bundle on the hook so its tips reach the middle of the tail.

10. Tie in the underwing at the position determined in the previous step, and trim the waste.

11. For the wings, cut two slips of matching turkey-feather sections from the left and right side of the stem, each one hook-gap wide. Put them together so the good sides are facing out. Set them on the underwing so the tips curve toward each other and meet over the middle of the tail.

12. Tie in the wing sections as you did the tail: Make two loose loops, and then hold the sections while releasing the loops. Position the wing above the underwing, not down in it.

13. Cut the waste off the forward part of the wing sections and bind down the stubs.

14. Cut a bundle of deer hair for a collar, and comb out the underfur.

Material Tip

Hair stacks much more easily when the underfur is removed.

15. After stacking, set the bundle on the hook so the tips extend the length of the body.

16. Spin the deer hair as in the instructions for Dave's Hopper, Step 27.

17. Cut, comb, and spin a second bunch of deer hair in front of the first. (No need to stack this bunch, as it will be trimmed into a head.)

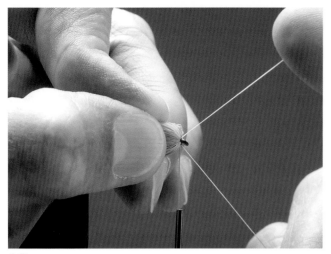

18. Pull the deer hair back, exposing the hook eye, and whip finish.

20. Gradually round the corners of the head, continuing until you have a bullet-shaped head, again taking care not to cut off the collar.

19. Remove the fly from the vise, trim the bottom of the head flat—taking care not to trim the collar—and then continue trimming the head into a cube.

21. The finished Muddler Minnow. This is one of those patterns that takes some practice to master. Tying a few in a row will help you get the feel for mounting the wings and working with the deer hair.

Appendix

WHIP FINISH

The whip finish is the standard method of tying off thread when a fly is complete, or in some cases, midway through a pattern. It forms a knot so secure that no head cement is required. Most accomplished fly tiers do the whip finish by hand rather than with a tool simply because it's faster and means one less gadget to pick up. Essentially, it involves making a loop with two fingers, then rolling and flipping this loop over the hook eye repeatedly to lock the thread over itself.

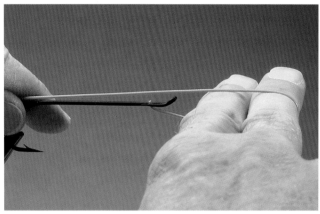

2. Maintaining tension on the thread with your bobbin hand, roll the two fingers clockwise . . .

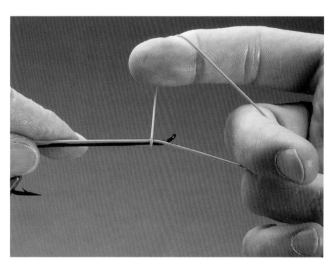

3. . . . and continue to roll, now bending the middle finger forward, creating a loop and trapping the thread behind the eye of the hook.

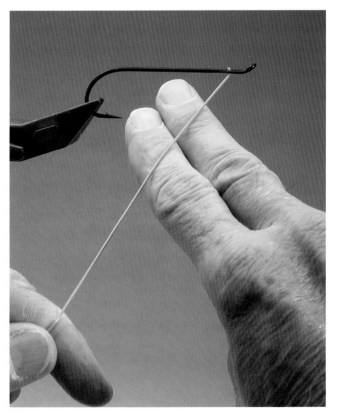

1. Pull about 8 inches of thread from your bobbin and position the index and middle finger of your working hand underneath the thread, as shown.

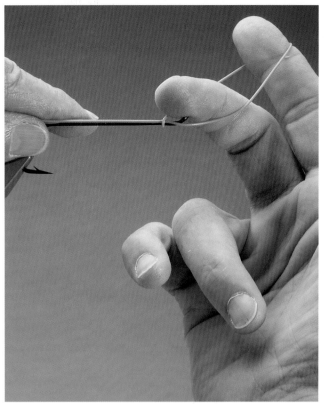

4. Continue rotating your hand—note that the palm of your working hand is now facing you—sliding the loop over the eye with your middle finger.

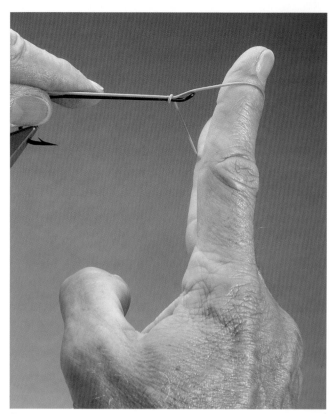

6. Roll your middle finger down, bringing the loop back toward the near side of the hook.

5. You have now closed the thread over itself.

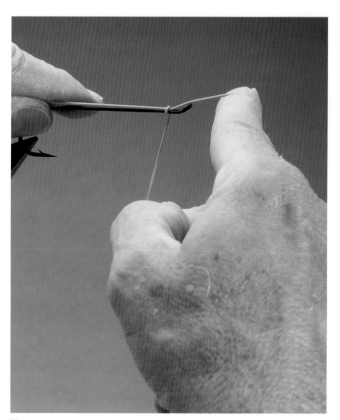

7. Roll your middle finger toward you while holding the thread straight out over the eye of the hook with your index finger.

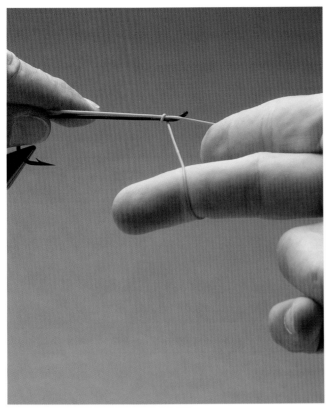

8. Hold tension on the loop with your middle finger.

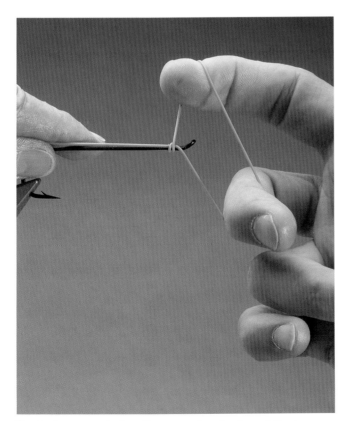

9. Swing your index finger under the leg of the loop being held by the middle finger, and raise it over the shank. This completes the first turn of the whip finish.

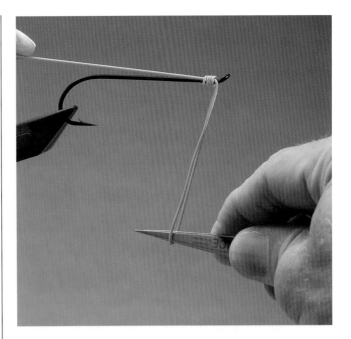

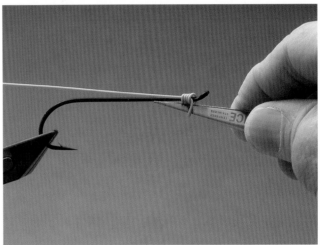

10. Repeat steps 3 through 7 four more times. Slip your fingers out of the loop and insert the point of your scissors.

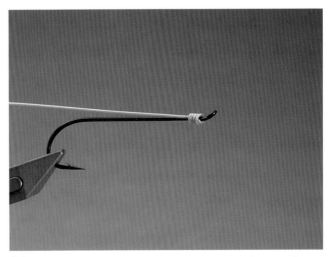

11. With your bobbin hand pulling thread away from the hook, tighten the loop.

X-WRAP

The X-wrap is a very simple method of locking wings perpendicular to the hook shaft. It is a key technique for attaching the wings in spent spinner patterns, and is also useful as the first step in tying a parachute wing-post to the hook.

1. Holding the thread perpendicular to the hook, position the wing material over the tie-in point.

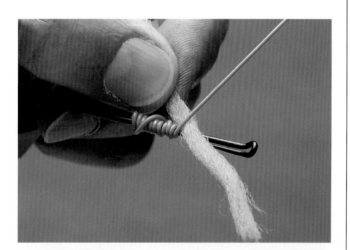

2. Make the fist wrap over the near wing.

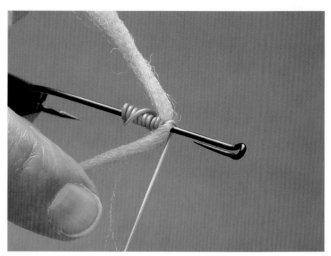

3. Pull the near wing rearward . . .

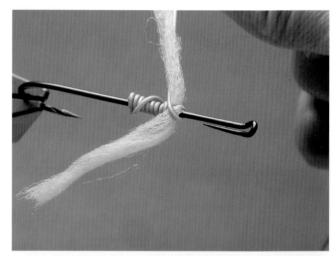

4. . . . and wrap over it and then behind the far wing.

5. Bring the thread under the near wing . . .

7. Bring the thread under the hook and back over to complete the X-wrap and lock the wings in position, perpendicular to the hook.

6. . . . and then over the hook and in front of the far wing.

Resources

BOOKS

Basic Fly Tying, Jon Rounds, ed. Stackpole Books.
Master tier Wayne Luallen demonstrates seven basic patterns in step-by-step sequences that leave nothing out.

Essential Trout Flies, Dave Hughes. Stackpole Books.
A valuable and handy condensation of *Trout Flies*, with the author's favorite patterns and variations.

The Fly Fisher's Illustrated Dictionary, Darrel Martin. Lyons Press.
A handy reference to fly-tying and fly-fishing terms, with many historical notes on their evolution.

The Fly Tier's Benchside Reference, Ted Leeson and Jim Schollmeyer. Amato Books.
The definitive reference for tying technique, tools, and materials.

Good Flies, John Gierach. Lyons Press.
This is the most tying-focused book from Gierach, who is known more for anecdotal works, like the classic *Trout Bum*. With recipes and detailed notes on his favorite patterns and their development.

Guide to Fly Tying, Dick Talleur. Stackpole Books.
A thick, comprehensive guide to tying, including basics and beyond.

Inside Fly Tying, Dick Talleur. Stackpole Books.
A veteran tier shares "100 tips for solving the trickiest fly-tying problems." The tips are shown in context, as part of the step-by-step instructions for fifteen patterns.

The Soft-Hackled Fly and *The Soft-Hackled Fly Addict*, Sylvester Nemes. Stackpole Books.
These two books are must-reads for anyone interested in the rediscovery and development of soft-hackled flies in the twentieth century.

Spring Creeks, Mike Lawson. Stackpole Books.
A big, beautiful book that delivers a wealth of information on choosing and fishing patterns for spring creeks, from Montana to Pennsylvania. With recipes.

Terrestrials, Harrison Steeves and Ed Koch. Stackpole Books.
A standard reference, with entomology, tying, and fishing notes.

Trout Flies, Dave Hughes. Stackpole Books.
Still the most comprehensive and reliable reference on trout fly patterns, this tome is a good choice to anchor any fly-tying library, no matter the size.

Tying Flies with CDC, Leon Links. Stackpole Books.
Originally published in Europe, where CDC was discovered as a tying material, this book includes a history of the development of CDC patterns, along with many recipes you won't find elsewhere.

Tying Small Flies, Ed Engle. Stackpole Books.
A comprehensive guide from the small-fly guru of the West. Includes a detailed examination of hooks and thread, along with step-by-step instructions for dozens of patterns, from midge pupae to tricos to ants.

DVDS

Basic Fly Tying, with Marvin Nolte. Stackpole Books.
This two-DVD set shows every step of the seven patterns in the book.

Beyond Basic Fly Tying, with Marvin Nolte. Stackpole Books.
The companion to this book.

Stackpole Basics

All the Skills and Tools You Need to Get Started

- Straightforward, expert instruction on a variety of crafts, hobbies, and sports
- Step-by-step, easy-to-follow format
- Current information on equipment and prices for the beginner
- Full-color photography and illustrations
- Convenient lay-flat spiral binding

BASIC FLY TYING
$19.95, 88 pages,
300 color photos, 35 illustrations,
978-0-8117-2473-9

BASIC FLY FISHING
$19.95, 120 pages,
180 color photos, 56 illustrations,
978-0-8117-3303-8

BASIC CANOEING
$16.95, 128 pages,
150 color photos, 40 illustrations,
978-0-8117-2644-3

BASIC KAYAKING
$19.95, 96 pages,
185 color photos, 35 illustrations,
978-0-8117-3210-9

Available at your favorite retailer,
or from Stackpole Books at (800) 732-3669

STACKPOLE BOOKS

www.stackpolebooks.com